J'lolade Erinkitola

THE
BLUE·CHIP
GRADUATE

A Four-Year College Plan
for Career Success

BILL OSHER, Ph.D., &
SIOUX HENLEY CAMPBELL

PEACHTREE PUBLISHERS, LTD.

Published by
PEACHTREE PUBLISHERS, LTD.
494 Armour Circle, N.E.
Atlanta, Georgia 30324

Manufactured in the United States of America

1st printing

Library of Congress Catalog Card Number 86-63534

ISBN 0-934601-19-4

Dedicated with much love and pride to Chris,
who is living proof that it works
                                    —LWO

Lovingly dedicated to Joshua and Ian,
each a Blue-Chipper in his own way
                                    —SHC

CONTENTS

APPENDICES

THE
BLUE·CHIP
GRADUATE

Foreword:

What Is a Blue-Chip Graduate?

We work at the Georgia Institute of Technology. Georgia Tech has an outstanding reputation in the corporate world. Our placement center does a booming business getting the IBMs and the GEs together with our graduating seniors. Yet even a Tech graduate may have to hustle for good job offers. And if some of our graduates are having a hard time, what about graduates from less prestigious colleges? Or students with less marketable majors?

This book grew out of our contact with disillusioned seniors and recent graduates who were struggling to get jobs in a highly competitive market. Why should bright young men and women with training in business, science, or engineering have trouble finding employment?

As we talked with more and more of them, we began to see a pattern. Most were incredibly naive about what it takes to get a good job. And in their naiveté, they had wandered passively and aimlessly for four years. They had done enough to get their degree. Yet, in a sense, they had sleepwalked through their college education.

We do our best to help these students, but we've found that it's a lot easier to teach someone to swim before they fall overboard. We're betting you want to be ready for the deep end of the pool when you finish college, that you want to launch a challenging career that has a future and not be forced to accept some job that leads nowhere.

You want to be a blue-chip graduate. The blue chips on the poker table are worth the most. Blue-chip stocks are the most valuable. Blue-chip athletes are the most heavily recruited. And blue-chip graduates get the best jobs and have the brightest futures.

You don't become a blue-chipper by accident. It takes hard work, but it takes more than just hard work. You've got to have a plan. This book gives you the plan. It tells you how to plan for success beginning the first day you set foot on a campus.

1
What College Students Want — Job$

How would you like to get through college and walk right into the job of your dreams? It's not impossible. There are a select few who do it. And you can become one of them. We've written this book to show you how.

If you're a college student or about to become one, the odds are that you're preoccupied with your career, practical, maybe somewhat materialistic. Why? Just a few years ago students were much more worried about society in general. Struggling up the corporate ladder was the last thing on their minds. So why are you so concerned about your personal future? Deciding on a marketable major? Thinking about a hot career? High income? Financial security?

Because you live in economically precarious times. No one knows for sure what's going to happen next. A few years ago our country struggled through the double whammy of a major recession and high inflation. In 1987, the economy is doing better and inflation is down. But we've become the biggest debtor nation in the world, and experts are telling us we've lost our competitive edge. In 1986 the average college graduate left the campus over $8,000 in debt. Yet the prospects for financial aid for college students appear to be dimming. If you're going into hock to get your degree, you'd like some assurance that some day you'll have your financial head above the water.

If you're just out of high school, you probably haven't thought much about buying a home, but you may have an older brother or sister who has complained about not being able to afford one. It's just possible that brother or sister has come back to live with the family. More men and women in their twenties are being forced by economics to do just that. It's a state of affairs that is usually less than perfect for all concerned.

Whoever you are, in the back of your mind you know you'd like to be able to buy or rent a safe, comfortable place after graduation. Well, lots of luck, because unless you hustle and plan, you probably won't be able to live as well as you did growing up.

Your parents probably spent one week's pay out of their monthly income on housing. Now, owning or renting can cost 30 to 40 percent of a family's income. In some instances, 50 percent. That doesn't leave much for food, clothing, and transportation. And less for luxuries or fun. In some parts of the country, four hundred-square-foot homes are being built. The house you grew up in may have been four or five times that size—or more. But, today, the smaller home is all many people can afford.

A member of your family may have gone without a job for a while. If so, you know how stressful unemployment can be. In fact, for every additional 1 percent of unemployment nationally, the national suicide rate goes up 4 percent. Even if joblessness hasn't touched you personally, you've seen the despairing faces on TV. People wanting jobs and not finding them. Or finding jobs that don't pay enough to live on. And bring little personal satisfaction.

Chances are you've heard your parents complain about their work. If you've been employed, you probably know firsthand how stifling the wrong job can be. Being underpaid or underchallenged can take its toll over the years. So can working under the latest incarnation of Attila the Hun. Yet career expert Tom Jackson suggests that as many as 80 percent of the American work force are seriously dissatisfied with their jobs.

You'd like something better.

Economists note that bankruptcies are up. So are home mortgage foreclosures and business failures. A 7 percent rate of unemployment used to be intolerable. Today, it's just the way things are. If people are being laid off, you can be sure that the companies that let them go are having a hard time too. So it's not surprising that American business has responded by getting more competitive. One way that employers compete is through more selective hiring. They're looking for blue-chip candidates first. In many instances, first and last.

Whether you're eighteen or thirty-eight, you know good jobs are scarce. You also know that without a good job, your life will be harder. That's why today's college student is practical, career-minded, materialistic.

Alexander Astin's annual survey of college freshmen has for several years now revealed that about three out of four go to college to get a better job. Two out of three say that making more money is a top reason.

In a 1984 survey of college administrators, the *Chronicle of Higher Education* reported that two-thirds believed that students were becoming more interested in their careers. They saw students becoming more grade-conscious and said that more students were flocking to career counseling and placement services.

More students are going into business and engineering. Why? Because they believe that's where the jobs are and where the money is. (Of course, this influx of students will eventually make competition stiffer in these fields.) More students have already started their own businesses, some of them not so small. More schools offer courses on starting and owning a business. Those courses have proved to be highly popular.

So what's the big revelation, you might be thinking. You may not be able to rattle off the precise statistics, but you've talked all this over with your friends, you've seen the news. Or maybe you've simply checked your own bank statement.

DREAMS, NOT GOALS

The point we want to make is that today's practical, bottom-line-oriented, career-minded college student isn't really so practical after all. Students don't realize what it takes to be successful. Consequently, many of their expectations are unrealistic. Most have no plan or map to guide them to their goals for professional success. In fact, when pressed, most are unable to come up with clear, concrete goals. They have dreams rather than goals, and dreams are notoriously more elusive.

In 1985 the employment firm Challenger, Gray, and Christmas surveyed some thirty-one thousand graduating college seniors. Their results suggested that over half would get out of college without jobs. Over a third didn't take advantage of their college's placement service. One-fourth of those who did still hadn't found work.

Many entering freshmen don't even have a clear idea of how to succeed academically. In a 1985 survey conducted at Penn State, most students predicted higher grades in college than they had made in high school. Four of five expected these high grades while studying fewer than twenty hours a week. Moreover, the majority of the students were found to have only marginal study skills. Students in two-year associate degree programs were found to be the most unrealistic of all.

The same survey showed students to be equally hazy on their choices of major and career. Only 13 percent said they knew much about their major. Only 14 percent had participated in activities related to their chosen careers.

Students today, then, have high aspirations, but they're low in the strategy department. And upon graduation they will face a business community that has had to develop strategies to cope with an increasingly competitive world. The anxieties that have fueled student aspirations are in response to real-world competition and belt-tightening. That's because today we live in a global market place, not just a national one.

General Motors has to compete with Toyota and Volkswagen as well as Ford and Chrysler. Our steel industry has to compete with Brazil's steel industry. American textiles, with those in Korea and Taiwan. Massachusetts Institute of Technology economist Lester Thurow notes that just thirty years ago the United States led the world in manufacturing almost every important consumer and industrial product. Now, we lead in virtually none.

LEAN AND MEAN

Business today has to be lean and mean. That was the phrase that kept cropping up as we researched this book. A corporate headhunter notes that "After the economic recession of 1980-82, corporations cut out the dead wood. People who had worked for a company for ten or twenty years were phased out." Lean and mean.

An outplacement counselor sees corporate employees having a much more difficult time moving up: "There will be fewer managers. More moves will be horizontal instead of vertical." Lean and mean.

A business writer sees "corporations interviewing at fewer colleges and universities. It just doesn't pay them to recruit at the weaker schools." Lean and mean.

A director of a major college placement center sees recruiters today "conducting much more demanding interviews with graduating seniors, probing for reasons to reject instead of looking for reasons to accept. It used to be a plant trip probably meant a job offer. That's not true anymore." Lean and mean.

In other words, one of the main ways American businesses compete is by hiring only the best new talent. We'll say it again. *Recruiters are looking for blue-chip graduates.* If you don't have the right stuff, you may well have to settle for leftovers. In fact, you need not only to have the right stuff, but also to have the marketing skills to prove it to employers.

The same is true in order to gain admission into graduate programs and professional schools. An admissions director of a top MBA program says she expects applicants to have a good academic record in a rigorous undergraduate program, to have some solid professional experience, and to have clear career goals.

In fact, competition has become so widespread that it is starting to affect even our much maligned public education system. It is finally beginning to dawn on the American people that we won't be able to compete with Japanese technology if our twelfth graders continue to know less mathematics than their ninth graders. So teachers' colleges are under pressure to raise their standards. Classroom teachers' pay raises may soon be made on the basis of merit.

THE VIRGIN GRADUATE

We found students who did not have clear career objectives. They wanted "a challenging position leading to management," but they couldn't describe that position or the skills it would require. They were preoccupied with what employers could do for them rather than figuring out what they could do for employers.

They didn't know what employers really wanted. They hadn't analyzed their own abilities and goals, so they couldn't say what they had to offer.

Some couldn't write well or speak articulately. Many had no career-related work experience. They frequently weren't acquainted with the opportunities in their own majors. They had built up no network of contacts. They didn't know any professors who would write them a strong recommendation. They lacked leadership experience.

Virtually none of them knew how the process of looking for a job really works. They frequently failed to research the companies that were interviewing them. Many were so ill at ease during interviews that they made poor impressions on corporate recruiters. They didn't know how to sell themselves to an employer.

In a student generation that's supposed to be comfortable with the business world, many graduates violated every basic business principle. They hadn't anticipated what employers wanted in a graduate. In other words, they hadn't surveyed the market. Because they hadn't surveyed the market, they couldn't develop a highly marketable product. Instead, they had squandered golden opportunities during their college years. And, finally, they had very little idea of how to market themselves, which is the only product anyone really has to offer.

WHAT THIS BOOK IS ABOUT

You have dreams of professional success, but you probably don't have a game plan for achieving it. This book gives you the plan, step by step, through four years of college. Follow the plan, and you will learn:

1. what employers want;
2. how to go through college so that you'll graduate with what employers want;
3. how to convince employers that you've got what they want.

And then you yourself will be a blue-chip graduate.

GET YOUR MONEY'S WORTH FROM THIS BOOK

First of all, USE it. Don't just read over it once and then forget it. Take the tests. Do the exercises. Complete the checklists. Read the appendices too; they're important. And this includes the list of suggested readings. It's also there for a reason. We planned *Blue-Chip* to be your four-year guide to success, a resource you can turn to time and again while you're in college. Here's one system for making it work for you:

1. Read the chapter highlights listed at the end of each chapter. Do this quickly and with as few interruptions as possible. This will give you a rough idea of what the book will cover.

2. Review the Master Plan on the following page. This will show you what you need to accomplish and give you a time frame for doing it.

3. Study the detailed Master Plan in Appendix I. As you go over each year, assess your status. The first year is called the freshman year for obvious reasons. If you are a sophomore or above and have not met all the preceding requirements, consider yourself a freshman blue-chipper.

4. Read the entire book. Do only those exercises and checklists suitable for your stage of blue-chip development. Follow the principles outlined in the book. Make use of the suggested additional readings as they become relevant to your needs.

5. Assess yourself at the end of each blue-chip year by doing the quiz in Appendix II, "Take Stock In Yourself." If you scored poorly, follow the instructions for adding to your blue-chip stock at the bottom of the quiz. If your score is satisfactory, transfer it to the "Blue-Chip Portfolio," Appendix III.

6. Watch your stock rise in the "Blue-Chip Portfolio" until you are a blue-chip graduate.

MASTER PLAN

FRESHMAN
Develop organizational skills Learn and practice study skills Seek career counseling Assess functional skills and set goals Investigate cooperative plan, internships, or career-related employment Learn stress management skills

SOPHOMORE
Declare major Join professional association Develop job-search skills Secure career-related employment

JUNIOR
Seek leadership positions Research specialized areas of your chosen field Research key corporations Research functional employment areas Research graduate or professional schools of your choice

SENIOR
Take graduate or professional school entrance exams Apply to graduate or professional schools Arrange for interviews through campus placement office Write a winning resume Research target corporations Get references Master the interviewing process Take plant trips or visit grad schools Evaluate offers

CONGRATULATIONS!
BEGIN YOUR BLUE-CHIP CAREER

2

What Employers Want— Blue-Chip Graduates

W hat do employers want?

A lot.

Remember, we live in a highly competitive world. The job you get when you graduate depends largely on how close you come to being an employer's ideal candidate. This is true whether you're shooting for a management position with Exxon or a job selling shoes in the local department store. It also applies if you hope to be admitted into a graduate or professional school.

You have just a few years to develop the skills that employers expect. It is extremely important, therefore, that you know what those skills are. By knowing what blue-chip graduates look like, you can greatly increase your chances of becoming one.

SALLY KOWALSKI

Campus Box 0000   Atlanta, GA 30032   (404) 894-0000

OBJECTIVE:

Seek an **administrative** position in a **health care organization** using my background in psychology, management and computers

EDUCATION:

FULTON UNIVERSITY   GPA: 3.2/4.0
B.A. Psychology   6/87
Concentration in Health Care Management

> **COURSEWORK:** Applied Psychology, Psychological Assessment, Organizational Psychology, Analysis of Health Care Systems, Health Care Marketing, Issues in Health Care Management, Legal Aspects of Health Care, Statistics

> **HONORS AND ACTIVITIES: Dean's List;** vice-president, American Hospital Association (student chapter); volunteer, Campus Crisis Center; financed **100%** of college expenses

SKILLS:

Administrative: Coordinated fund-raising events to offset budget deficit for Campus Crisis Center

Leadership: Directed monthly student meetings of American Hospital Association; served as liaison between AHA and campus administration

Computer: Proficient in BASIC, dBASEIII, Lotus 1-2-3, and Volks-writer; working experience with CDC Cyber and IBM PC

EXPERIENCE:
LANGDALE MEMORIAL HOSPITAL AND NURSING HOME
Intern   6/86-3/87

> **Program Management:** Collaborated on the development and implementation of an "Adopt a Grandparent" program; successful marketing strategy resulted in 80% placement rate of nursing home residents

ADULT SERVICES DEPARTMENT OF PENSIONS AND SECURITIES
Interviewer   9/83-5/86

> **Communication:** Interviewed applicants and referred them to appropriate person or agency

REFERENCES FURNISHED UPON REQUEST

A RECRUITER LOOKS AT CANDIDATES

Every year corporate recruiters scour college campuses, looking for blue-chip graduates. Before you know it, they will be examining your resume and probing you with tough questions to see if you qualify. Let's sit in with a recruiter at work so you'll know what to expect.

He spends his day in a small cubicle, furnished with a modest desk and two or three chairs. The offices and furniture are interchangeable from one placement center to the next. Sometimes it seems to him that the candidates are interchangeable as well. Dressed conservatively and armed only with his questions and powers of observation, he pulls out a stack of resumes from his briefcase. He knows he will talk with many more candidates than his company has jobs to offer.

He takes a sip of coffee from a styrofoam cup and looks at the resume of the candidate he's going to interview in a few minutes. This is how he appraises it.

OBJECTIVE:

Seek an **administrative** position in a **health care organization** using my background in psychology, management and computers

The first thing he looks at is the JOB OBJECTIVE. If Sally's goals don't match what his company has to offer, there's not much point in considering her very seriously. "So far, so good," he thinks. "We're expanding, and we're going to need a lot of entry-level managers. She's computer literate, and she wants to work in our kind of ball park."

EDUCATION:

FULTON UNIVERSITY   GPA: 3.2/4.0
B.A. Psychology   6/87
Concentration in Health Care Management

    COURSEWORK: Applied Psychology, Psychological Assessment, Organizational Psychology, Analysis of Health Care Systems, Health Care Marketing, Issues in Health Care Management, Legal Aspects of Health Care, Statistics

    HONORS AND ACTIVITIES: Dean's List; vice-president, American Hospital Association (student chapter); volunteer, Campus Crisis Center; financed **100%** of college expenses

EDUCATION usually comes next on a student's resume. A more experienced individual would probably list her work history next. "A 3.2. Not outstanding, but solid enough. And even though she's a Psych major, her concentration gives her the background she'd need for our organization." He underlines some of her courses with a felt pen.

When he sees that, in addition to Dean's List grades, she's been an officer in a health care professional organization and was a volunteer in a crisis center, he nods his head. "This is what we're looking for. Someone with people skills as well as some technical know-how. Probably a leader. Apparently knows what she wants, and is going to get it."

SKILLS:

Administrative: Coordinated fund-raising events to offset budget deficit for Campus Crisis Center

Leadership: Directed monthly student meetings of American Hospital Association; served as liaison between AHA and campus administration

Computer: Proficient in BASIC, dBASEIII, Lotus 1-2-3, and Volks-writer; working experience with CDC Cyber and IBM PC

Glancing over the SKILLS section, our recruiter notes that Sally would be able to use her computer skills in program evaluation, accounting, and annual report writing. "And if she wants to get into management, she's already shown a flair for getting people to accomplish things."

EXPERIENCE:

LANGDALE MEMORIAL HOSPITAL AND NURSING HOME
Intern   6/86-3/87

Program Management: Collaborated on the development and implementation of an "Adopt a Grandparent" program; successful marketing strategy resulted in 80% placement rate of nursing home residents

ADULT SERVICES DEPARTMENT OF PENSIONS AND SECURITIES
Interviewer   9/83-5/86

Communication: Interviewed applicants and referred them to appropriate person or agency

When our recruiter looks over Sally's EXPERIENCE, he first thinks to himself that he's glad to see a student who has some. Many don't. Grades and academic honors are fine, but can a student cut it in the real world? Meet deadlines? Solve an employer's problems? And since Sally had an internship, she has experience that relates to her career. To the company she's interviewing with. Flipping hamburgers for Hardee's doesn't look nearly as good as developing programs for Humana Hospital. "She's got some relevant work experience. She's taken on projects and seen them through. If she'll visit the home office, one of our executives can determine just exactly how pertinent her experience is for our needs.

"She doesn't list her REFERENCES, but I'd be willing to bet she'll get some strong recommendations from top people. She definitely looks like a blue-chipper. She's sharp, has experience, has communication skills, and is hard working. Now, let's see if she looks as good in person as she does on paper."

THE INTERVIEW

Our recruiter walks down a hall and into a reception area where over a dozen dressed-for-success young men and women wait expectantly. Conversations end suddenly, and eyes turn toward the recruiter, who calls out Sally Kowalski's name. A small woman in a dark gray suit folds the newspaper she's been reading, stands up, and offers her hand.

As he escorts Sally down the hall, he's thinking that she's already making a good impression. An infectious smile, a firm handshake, and good eye contact. She said she had looked forward to meeting the representative from HealthCo, and it felt like she meant it.

He invites her to sit down and takes his own seat. They chat for a few minutes about entertainment in Atlanta and discover a shared enthusiasm for the Braves' Dale Murphy and a bewilderment about the rest of the lineup. She seems quite at ease, so it's time to get down to business. He asks her to comment on her professional goals.

She says that she has given a lot of thought to that issue. She believes she can best clarify her goals by explaining how they evolved. Since she thought of herself as a "people-person," she majored in psychology. To help pay her way through college, she got a part-time job as an interviewer screening and referring applicants at a welfare agency. Although she got some satisfaction from helping people find the right department, she didn't really see any position in the agency that she would want to make a career of.

While she was still a freshman, she became a volunteer with the campus crisis center. She liked going through the training, learning the listening skills and all, but she found that she didn't really like working with people who were highly upset. She began to wonder if psychology was really for her, but she had no idea what else to consider. She got some career counseling and learned that managerial and administrative work might be compatible with her interests and abilities. After thoroughly researching her options, she decided to stick with psychology, but she would add on a concentration in health care management. The idea of helping people get good medical care through program development and management really excited her.

Rather than severing her relationship with the campus crisis center, she shifted to an administrative role. Seeing a fund-raising project through to its successful completion gave her a great deal of satisfaction and confirmed to her that she was on the right track. Her grades picked up after she saw how her college coursework could prepare her for a challenging and rewarding career.

On her internship she worked on a project to serve a geriatric population. She found that interviewing the patients was fascinating, and it made her feel good. Eventually, she'd like to develop other geriatric programs. She had taken some computer courses before interning, and that turned out to be a godsend. Langdale Hospital kept all their records and did all their statistical analyses with computers.

She summarizes by saying she wants to be in the program development area of health care. Eventually she wants to do some more work that will help geriatric populations.

Her statement is well thought out and confidently presented. He's also struck by the evident concern she feels for her patients. The recruiter is definitely convinced that Sally will accomplish these goals, if not for HealthCo, then for someone else. He asks her to elaborate on how Langdale Hospital met with such success on their "Adopt a Grandparent" program. She enthusiastically and concisely outlines the various components of the project and her own role as an intern. Her responsibilities were, in fact, considerable, which is why she accepted the position over a better paying internship with an insurance company that offered less challenging work. Only ten minutes into the interview, and he's thoroughly impressed with her communication skills.

The recruiter asks Sally to discuss her strengths. She pauses thoughtfully and mentions three: she considers herself to be a good communicator, a good organizer, and a hard worker. Then she backs up her statement with facts from her personal history. She cites her experience interviewing for the welfare board, counseling with the crisis center, and chairing committees with the American Hospital Association. She discusses how she balances her academics and her extracurricular activities. She describes how she organized various projects she was responsible for. And, finally, she has made good grades, worked part-time, and been active on campus, and has squeezed in time for fun.

When the recruiter asks her about her weaknesses, she says she has to watch herself or she gets impatient with others. She likes things to be done right, but she's learning that different people contribute in different ways and at different speeds. She adds that working with geriatric patients has also taught her to be more patient.

It is obvious to the recruiter that Sally has thought out her answers to the standard interview questions. He's already convinced enough of her potential to offer her an interview at the home office. Still, the skeptic in him wonders just how thorough she really is. He asks her his final standard question. "How do you think you could contribute to HealthCo, and why would you want to work for us?"

"Dr. Cromwell was one of my professors," she answers, "and he's done a lot of consulting for HealthCo. He mentioned to some of us that you will be doing a lot more in the way of geriatric work in the future. He also said that you have a much higher percentage of non-physicians in middle- and upper-management. Those were the two main factors that led me to consider HealthCo very seriously.

"The more I found out about HealthCo, the better the company looked to me. HealthCo has been a leader in keeping medical costs down and still maintaining a high quality of service. Your annual report says that you'll be devoting 25 percent of your budget to developing geriatric programs. I'd like to be a part of that division as it's starting up."

The recruiter smiles and starts wrapping up the interview. Sally has looked at more than the usual corporate literature available to students in most placement centers. She has researched the company thoroughly. He tells her she can expect further contact from HealthCo and thanks her for an interesting interview. If more candidates were like her, his job would be a lot easier.

Several hours later our recruiter is looking at another resume, that of Sam Dresden. He slowly shakes his head.

OBJECTIVE: A challenging and responsible position with a chance for advancement in a growth industry

The JOB OBJECTIVE tells him nothing. What kind of challenging and responsible position? What sort of advancement?

EDUCATION:	**FULTON UNIVERSITY**	
	Atlanta, GA	GPA: 2.8/4.0
	B.A. Psychology	
	Minor in French	June 1987
	MERRIMAC COLLEGE	
	Dawsonville, GA	GPA: 3.1/4.0
	European Studies Curriculum	6/85-12/85
	MIDDLETON JUNIOR COLLEGE	
	Atlanta, GA	GPA: 3.3/4.0
	A.S. Geography	9/83-6/85

Coursework: Abnormal Psychology, Social Psychology, Psychological Assessment, French I,I,III, Contour Mapping, Waters of the World, dBASE III, BASIC

Our recruiter moves on to EDUCATION and frowns. A fair GPA, but different schools and different curricula with no focus. If this resume had come in the morning mail, he would have dropped it in the wastebasket under his desk within ten seconds of picking it up. But he has an appointment with the candidate, so he quickly reviews the rest of the resume.

SAM DRESDEN

Campus Box 0001   Atlanta, Georgia 30332   (404) 894-1111

OBJECTIVE: A challenging and responsible position with a chance for advancement in a growth industry

EDUCATION: **FULTON UNIVERSITY**
Atlanta, GA   GPA: 2.8/4.0
  B.A. Psychology
    June 1987
  Minor in French

MERRIMAC COLLEGE
Dawsonville, GA   GPA: 3.1/4.0
  European Studies Curriculum   6/85-12/85

MIDDLETON JUNIOR COLLEGE
Atlanta, GA   GPA: 3.3/4.0
  A.S. Geography   9/83-6/85

Coursework: Abnormal Psychology, Social Psychology, Psychological Assessment, French I,I,III, Contour Mapping, Waters of the World, dBASE III, BASIC

WORK HISTORY:

Waiter   **TIPPINS RESTAURANT**   10/85-present
Responsible for servicing lunchtime shift at mostly capacity crowds

Bus Boy   **TIPPINS RESTAURANT**   7/85-9/85
Responsible for clearing tables, setting the tables, replenishing salad bar and washing bar glasses as needed; promoted to waiter after two months

Assistant   **MIGUEL'S TREE SURGERY**   (summers) 1983-84
Tree   Responsible for removing dead limbs and
Surgeon   fertilizing trees and shrubbery

INTERESTS: Computer graphics, backpacking, running, photography, drawing and reading

REFERENCES: Furnished upon request

WORK HISTORY:

Waiter	**TIPPINS RESTAURANT**	10/85-present
	Responsible for servicing lunchtime shift at mostly capacity crowds	
Bus Boy	**TIPPINS RESTAURANT**	7/85-9/85
	Responsible for clearing tables, setting the tables, replenishing salad bar and washing bar glasses as needed; promoted to waiter after two months	
Assistant Tree Surgeon	**MIGUEL'S TREE SURGERY** (summers) 1983-84	
	Responsible for removing dead limbs and fertilizing trees and shrubbery	

At least Sam has a WORK HISTORY. May even have put himself through school. That counts for something. But Sam doesn't relate his work to marketable skills or to a career path. Unless he wants to work in the company cafeteria. Or for groundskeeping.

INTERESTS: Computer graphics, backpacking, running, photography, drawing and reading

The recruiter glances at INTERESTS momentarily and then reluctantly heads out to get his candidate. Like the rest of the resume, Sam's interests don't show what he can do for HealthCo.

THE INTERVIEW

When he gets to the waiting area and announces Sam's name, the recruiter gets no response. He calls out the name louder. Nothing. Just as he checks his watch, a young man in a navy blue suit bursts through the door. "Would you be Mr. Dresden?" the recruiter asks dryly. "At your service," is the reply. The recruiter shakes his hand while Sam apologizes for being late. He had gotten hung up at work. "No problem," says the recruiter. But of course it is. This appointment had been made two weeks ago. He should have arranged to be on time.

When they finally sit down in the interview room Sam is perspiring heavily. He fumbles for a handkerchief. When he doesn't find one, he wipes the dampness off his forehead with the back of his hand. The recruiter leads him through the same set of questions that he posed to Sally. The results are quite different.

In response to the question about professional goals, Sam wants to know what HealthCo has available. He lists his strengths as being hard-working, ambitious, and a good communicator. He doesn't offer any evidence to support his claim, so the recruiter asks him to elaborate. Sam says he has paid his entire way through college. He has worked as many as twenty hours a week while being a full-time student. He wants something better in his future. He discusses how hectic his college years have been. The recruiter nods and begins to appreciate Sam a little more. He does get the feeling that Sam isn't afraid of work. And while his answers aren't well organized, he has a relaxed manner about him.

When asked to discuss his weaknesses, Sam draws a blank and makes a nervous joke about not really having any. The recruiter remains silent, giving Sam a chance to collect his thoughts. This only makes the candidate more anxious, and he begins to ramble on about how restless and bored he gets when confronted with mundane activities such as writing papers. The recruiter notes that he certainly hadn't anticipated the question. Plus the answer he gave was very negative. Would he have the patience to fill out his reports? Would he meet his deadlines?

The recruiter has pretty well already eliminated Sam. He gives him one last chance. "What could you contribute to our company, and why do you want to work for us?

Sam says that everybody knows about HealthCo, and he's always wanted to work for a major corporation. He has nothing more to add. Just as the recruiter suspected, Sam hasn't done his homework.

He doesn't know any more about HealthCo than the man on the street. Maybe less. He doesn't seem to know marketing from research from the fifty-yard line. He's not a bad kid, but he's out of his league. He doesn't know what he wants. He doesn't know what HealthCo wants. So naturally he can't sell himself.

Corporations pay recruiters to screen out weak candidates, not to provide a job placement service. An interviewer has no obligation to help lost applicants sort out their confusion. Yet Sam acts like he came for employment counseling instead of a job interview.

It's interesting that the recruiter thinks of Sam as a kid. In fact, he's a year older than Sally Kowalski and looks several years older than that. He thinks and acts like a kid though, while Sally conveyed an altogether professional image.

When we say "professional image," we're not talking about something superficial. It's not something you can fake on a resume or cover up with glib talk during an interview. Dressing for success won't get it either, if you haven't developed the real world skills and technical knowledge that employers demand.

The problem isn't that Sam majored in psychology instead of engineering or business. Many top executives have humanities or social science degrees (see Chapter 5). Nor is Sam without his selling points. He is ambitious, hard-working, and personable. But with neither focus nor direction, his strengths get lost in a confusing resume and a confused interview. He didn't know what he wanted out of college, so he wasn't able to get as much out of it as Sally.

WHAT THE EXPERTS SAY

We've taken you through two fictional job interviews. Were they realistic? Is that the way recruiters really think? In order to make sure, we asked a lot of people.

We asked recent graduates who were still going through their own job search. Ralph, an engineer who has had to settle for under-employment for almost a year now, says that every recruiter goes over three things: grades and courses, extracurricular activities, and work experience. "I was weak in all three areas, and I'm having to pay for it."

We talked with people who had finally landed their first career-related job. If they had it to do over, what would they do differently? Joan, who is a systems analyst in a bank, says, "I'd co-op or get an internship. I just wasn't ready for the business world. It's been a hard adjustment for me."

We asked recognized authorities what students should be doing while in college to get ready for the job market. Ken Blanchard, coauthor of the phenomenally successful *One Minute Manager*, had this to say: "One of the things that's in vogue now is entrepreneurial thinking. I think it's exciting for interviewers when kids can talk about some aspect of creating their own business and the initiative it took to start it. Or if they had some kind of position where they actually had subordinates.

"I would say to young people, 'Your lifeguarding and all your fun summers are fine, but it will cost you on your initial entry into a job. What employers would rather see is what kind of real-world issues you've had to deal with. What's your experience in selling and getting turned down? How do you deal with that? What kind of people have you supervised? Have you had to deal with any older employees when you're the young upstart?'"

We talked with a number of corporate recruiters. They said things like "career-related work experience. Those who have it learn much more from their courses." Another emphasized "having a clear job objective. And the only way they get it is by having actual experience in their field. They need to know the way a whole industry works. Or at least an entire division and the way the various jobs in it function. You just don't learn that from a textbook."

And we asked a representative from IBM what students should do to make themselves more attractive to his organization. "Tell them to get their grades up. We generally hire only the cream of the crop." Does IBM ever recruit anyone under a 3.0? "We have no cut-off. But a student with a low GPA had better look very strong in the other areas. And the 2.7 students we do hire are the ones with enough drive and self-confidence not to be scared off by our reputation for hiring only the best."

We sent out surveys to 250 Fortune 500 firms, asking them to "Rate the importance of the following characteristics which make a graduating college senior desirable as a job candidate." They rated each characteristic on a five-point scale. We assigned three points for each rating of "Very Important," two points to each rating of "Important," and one point for each rating of "Moderately Important." We subtracted a point for each rating of "Little Importance" and two points for each rating of "Not Important." The following table summarizes the responses of the eighty-one corporations who returned our survey:

RECRUITER SURVEY

CHARACTERISTIC	TOTAL POINTS
1. Speaking Well	206
2. Getting Along Well With Others	195
3. Hard Working	189
4. Analyzing Well	186
5. Expertise (Knowing Your Field Well)	185
6. Writing Well	181
7. Taking Initiative	180
8. Organizing Time, Data, Things Efficiently	175
9. Leadership	172
10. Major and Electives Taken	170
11. Work Experience	142
12. Having Clear Career Goals	141
13. Responding Well To Authority	130
14. Computer Skills	113
15. Reputation of College	101
16. Salesmanship	91
17. Negotiating Well	90
18. Good References and Contacts	74
19. Training, Supervision, Teaching Skills	20
20. Foreign Language	-83

So what do employers want? In today's competitive business world they want a lot. A blue-chipper has people skills and technical expertise. Real world experience and a solid academic record. How do you develop all this in four or five short years? Turn the page, because that's what the rest of this book is about.

SUMMARY

1. Anticipate stiff competition for good jobs when you graduate.
2. Employers look for blue-chip graduates. Here's what they expect:
    clear career goals;
    academic excellence;
    career-related work experience;
    campus involvement;
    knowledge of your field and industry;
    a willingness to work hard;
    the ability to get along with others;
    a match between their needs and your ability to contribute.
3. Now is the time to start developing these attributes.

3

How To Write A Term Paper, Coordinate Homecoming, & Still Have Time To Party

In 1956 the chairman of Great Britain's most prestigious retail firm, Marks & Spencer, happened to see two employees working late at night on inventory. Sir Simon Marks was disturbed. He didn't want to be a Scrooge who worked his people endless hours. He didn't want to pay a lot of overtime either. So he decided to streamline his system.

He ordered every piece of paper scrutinized. His guiding rule: "If in doubt, throw it out." Not only was time saved; over the following year 120 TONS of paper were eliminated. Even though retail floor space doubled, staff could be trimmed. Oh, yes, and *profits eventually increased 600 percent.*

Getting organized. Not the most glamorous notion to come down the pike. Or the most thrilling. But it is a fact of life for every successful business. Or business executive. Or blue-chip graduate. Remember Sally Kowalski and Sam Dresden? Who was organized? Who was going to get the fat offer?

Time is money in the business world. From the day you enter the work force, your professional life will be made up of a series of complex projects and deadlines. When corporations assess job candidates, one of the foremost qualities they look for is organizational ability. Can he juggle several projects? Can she establish priorities? Meet deadlines?

But you don't have to wait until graduation. If you attend a competitive college, organizational skills can make your survival a whole lot more likely. And they're absolutely essential if you expect to excel. If you want to be a blue-chip graduate, you've got to manage your time and resources.

Six Good Reasons To Get Organized
1. You'll make better grades.
2. You'll do better work.
3. You'll get better job offers.
4. Being organized is easier. The idea is to work smarter, not just harder.
5. It reduces stress. What good are a BMW and a yacht if you die of a heart attack at forty? Or get ulcers over final exams?
6. You'll have more time to party. Blue-chippers accomplish a lot, but they still have time for fun. The only way you can get everything done and still play is by managing your time and resources effectively.

MASTERING TIME

Suppose you ran a large department store. You'd need a plan, wouldn't you? And a plan is nothing more than goals in a time frame. Different merchandise for different times of the year. Planning for the Christmas season alone requires an incredible number of hours. What to sell? How to stock it and when to order it? Advertising, added part-time sales staff, beefed-up security, and so on. All this is decided many months before Santa sticks his beard on and stuffs a pillow under his red coat.

And it's the same for you as a student. Do you know which weeks in the semester are going to be your busiest? How many tests you'll have to take and papers you'll have to write? Do you know approximately how many pages you'll have to read in all your classes over the entire semester? You should. You can. And you soon will.

GETTING STARTED

The first step in time management is to set goals. The most important characteristic of high achievers is that they're goal directed—they know what they want (see Chapter 11). They've got clear goals, goals they can visualize. And they can see the steps that will take them to those goals. If you don't know where you're going, you're probably not going to get there.

You've got to get organized on paper. Otherwise, your plans may turn into dreams and never come true. A plan isn't a plan if it's not in writing. So says Peter Drucker, perhaps the world's leading authority on management. He's right. You've got to maintain daily, weekly, and semester schedules. It's a rare freshman who schedules everything on paper. It's a rarer executive who doesn't.

The first step is to set goals. Write them down. Then make a list of the activities that will get you to those goals. Prioritize those activities. Do them in order of importance

First, plan your semester (or quarter).

SEMESTER SCHEDULE					
	PSYCH 3 TESTS 1 PAPER FINAL 600pp TEXT	**MATH** 8 QUIZZES MIDTERM FINAL WEEKLY HW* 300pp TEXT	**HIST** 3 TESTS 1 PAPER FINAL 700pp TEXT	**BIOL** 4 TESTS MIDTERM FINAL 400pp TEXT	**LIT** MIDTERM 2 PAPERS FINAL 800pp TEXT
WEEK 1		*QUIZ, HW*			
WEEK 2		*QUIZ, HW*			
WEEK 3		*HW*		*TEST*	
WEEK 4	*TEST*	*QUIZ, HW*	*TEST*		
WEEK 5		*HW*			
WEEK 6		*QUIZ, HW*		*TEST*	
WEEK 7		*HW*			*PAPER*
WEEK 8	*TEST*	*MIDTERM, HW*	*TEST*	*MIDTERM*	*MIDTERM*
WEEK 9		*QUIZ, HW*			
WEEK 10		*HW*			
WEEK 11		*QUIZ, HW*		*TEST*	
WEEK 12		*HW*			
WEEK 13	*TEST*	*QUIZ, HW*	*TEST*		
WEEK 14	*PAPER*	*QUIZ, HW*	*PAPER*	*TEST*	*PAPER*
WEEK 15		*HW*			
WEEK 16	*FINAL*	*FINAL*	*FINAL*	*FINAL*	*FINAL*

*HOMEWORK

QUARTERLY SCHEDULE										
COURSE AND REQUIREMENTS	WEEK ONE	WEEK TWO	WEEK THREE	WEEK FOUR	WEEK FIVE	WEEK SIX	WEEK SEVEN	WEEK EIGHT	WEEK NINE	WEEK TEN
PSYCHOLOGY 3 TESTS 1 PAPER FINAL EXAM 400pp TEXT				*TEST*			*TEST*	*PAPER*		*FINAL EXAM*
MATH 5 QUIZZES MIDTERM FINAL EXAM HOMEWORK 200pp TEXT	*QUIZ* *HOME-WORK*	*QUIZ* *HOME-WORK*	 *HOME-WORK*	*QUIZ* *HOME-WORK*	*MID-TERM* *HOME-WORK*	 *HOME-WORK*	*QUIZ* *HOME-WORK*	*QUIZ* *HOME-WORK*	 *HOME-WORK*	*FINAL EXAM*
HISTORY 2 TESTS 1 PAPER FINAL EXAM 400pp TEXT				*TEST*			*TEST*	*PAPER*		*FINAL EXAM*
BIOLOGY 3 TESTS FINAL EXAM 400pp TEXT			*TEST*		*TEST*		*TEST*			*FINAL EXAM*
LITERATURE 1 TEST 2 PAPERS FINAL EXAM 400pp TEXT				*PAPER*	*TEST*			*PAPER*		*FINAL EXAM*

Most professors will hand out a syllabus or course outline early in the semester. Use the different syllabi to make up a calendar for the entire semester.

From this calendar several facts immediately become obvious. The student is responsible for covering twenty-eight hundred pages of textbook material. Additional reading will be required for the papers. If you assume the sixteenth week will be devoted to reviewing for finals, that figures out to be about 187 pages per week. About 27 pages a day if you count weekends. Thirty-seven, if you don't. The fourth, eighth, thirteenth, fourteenth, and sixteenth weeks are high demand weeks—when most of your papers and tests are scheduled. (Although the numbers will be different for a quarterly calendar, the principle is the same.)

If this were your calendar, it would be important for you to begin researching your papers that are due at the end of the semester during the ninth week. You'd organize and do most of your writing during the twelfth week. Otherwise, you'd be stuck with trying to dig up material on three topics and pulling it together at the last minute. Remember, you're going to be busy with two tests and a quiz during the thirteenth week.

You can see why a semester calendar is so important. But don't stop there. You've got to break up your semester goals into smaller, achievable tasks. You then schedule these tasks into your weeks and days. We suggest starting off with a weekly schedule that you adjust from day to day as the situation demands.

The first step in constructing a weekly schedule is to write down everything that is fixed. Sally Kowalski has done just that. She is signed up for sixteen hours of classes. She also works ten hours a week as an interviewer for a welfare agency so she can have some spending money. Assuming she sleeps eight hours a night and takes an hour for each meal, that uses up 105 of her 164 weekly hours. (Even though she is signed up for sixteen hours, she's in class eighteen. Biology adds up to six hours because of lab.) That leaves her just fifty-nine hours per week to get in everything else: laundry, exercise, dating, showers, errands, goofing off. Oh, yes, and studying. She's been advised to study two hours outside of class for each hour in class. So she figures she'll have to put in about thirty hours a week on the books. That leaves her about thirty hours for everything else.

Sally finally ended up scheduling twenty-four hours of study time. She thinks she can get by with that amount because she plans to be efficient. But she realizes she may have to adjust her plans. She has allotted herself about six hours a week to exercise. She knows she'll feel better if she does. She also plans to watch the nightly news most evenings after dinner and before she starts studying. Some nights she may go straight to the library and read the newspaper or *Newsweek* instead. On weeknights Sally plans to knock off studying by 10:30 or 11. She likes to wind down before going to bed by talking on the phone with her boyfriend, Chuck, or visiting with friends on the hall.

Sally is a psychology major. Early in the semester she decides to become involved in the Campus Crisis Center. She figures that will

SALLY'S WEEKLY SCHEDULE

	MON	TUES	WED	THUR	FRI	SAT	SUN
8AM	BREAKFAST						
9AM	MATH	LIT	MATH	LIT	MATH	BREAKFAST	
10AM	STUDY	PSYCH	STUDY	PSYCH	STUDY	EXERCISE	
11AM	HISTORY	PSYCH	HISTORY	PSYCH	HISTORY		
NOON	LUNCH						
1PM	BIOLOGY	BIOLOGY LAB	BIOLOGY	WORK	BIOLOGY		STUDY
2PM	STUDY		STUDY		WORK		
3 PM	WORK		WORK			STUDY	
4PM		EXERCISE		EXERCISE			
5PM							
6PM	DINNER						
7PM	CRISIS CENTER	NEWS	CRISIS CENTER	NEWS	NEWS		STUDY
8PM		STUDY		STUDY			
9PM	STUDY		STUDY				
10PM							
11PM	NEWS		NEWS				
12PM	BEDTIME						BEDTIME

OBLIGATIONS   FLEX TIME

help her get a feel for what psychology is all about. It will mean giving up only four hours a week, and she's been told she can get a fair amount of studying done while she's waiting for the hotline to ring.

She has thought about joining a sorority, but she's not sure if she can afford the time and money. She'll go through rush next semester and decide. She has planned Friday and Saturday nights to be free for recreation and seeing Chuck. She has left a few other weekend hours unscheduled. She knows they'll be easy to fill up with rest and relaxation. She also knows she may have to use some of this flex-time for studying as the semester picks up.

As you can see, Sally's schedule is a full one. If anything, we think it may be too full. It would be less stressful for her if she could cut back somewhere. For example, if she could manage it financially, it would probably make sense for her to drop her part-time work. She can get some career-related work experience through a co-op plan or on a summer internship. If Sally's finances require her to work while in school (which is quite common), she might consider taking a lighter academic load. Then again, she might be able to get by with fewer study hours.

She also would be better off if she put in some more flex-time or catch-up time. Assignments and projects have a way of taking longer than you anticipate. Things come up that throw schedules off. Keeping an hour open each day is a good idea. There will almost always be a need for it.

It is probably apparent that this is the schedule of an eighteen-year-old freshman. As busy as she is, she probably doesn't have to contend with all the demands on a single parent. Or on those who have to work full time to finance their education. See chapter 10 for tips on how such nontraditional students can get everything done and still maintain their sanity.

HINTS TO MAKE YOUR SCHEDULE WORK

1. Put down all the fixed items. Sally did this. She noted all her class time, sleep time, meal time, and work time. Then she added study and recreation and miscellaneous. Even had it been *M*A*S*H* reruns. If she watched regularly, she would have made a note of it.

2. Prioritize every day. Throughout your professional life there will be more things to do than you can do well. Successful people don't necessarily get the most things done, but they invariably get the most important things done.

3. Schedule something fun everyday. One of the reasons people don't follow their own plans is because they make out schedules that are

D. E.

unrealistically demanding. Sally has included several workouts that she looks forward to each week. She has arranged her time so that she stops working every night at no later than 11:00. Then she can read or socialize. Weekends include even more social and fun time. A colleague of ours puts it this way: "All work and no play makes Jack a fool."

4. Work first. Then reward yourself with play. The typical student avoids work all day, then begins to buckle down about eight or nine o'clock. Or even later. During the day, tomorrow's paper or test was probably weighing on the student's mind, interfering with the television he was watching, spoiling the bull session he was involved in. He didn't really enjoy his play. Now he's faced with having to study past midnight. What he's done is punish himself for having played.

Get the more difficult subjects out of the way first. Or the less interesting ones. Do them while you're fresh. Save your favorite subject for later, kind of as a reward.

5. Study between classes. As simple as this is, it puts you ahead of the pack. Instead of going to the student center after class, or your room, or the snack bar, go to the library. Once you're there, about all there is to do is study. A successful architect once told me that one of his most productive college semesters was one in which he busted his buns every weekday from eight to six. By working all day, he had time to goof off at night.

6. Don't schedule long blocks of study time. Research shows that you will learn more if you study, say, one and one-half hours in the morning, two hours in the afternoon, and another one and one-half hours in the evening than if you try to study five straight hours at night. This is because the last few hours of extended study time are less effective because of fatigue and boredom. If you do have to study in longer blocks of time, break up your routine by alternating subjects. Take breaks periodically. Think of a four-hour block of time as four fifty-minute blocks separated by short breaks.

7. Reward yourself. Have a snack or call a friend after accomplishing something modest. Buy a record after finishing up something big.

PLANNING FOR LIFE

We're not against good luck, but we think it usually comes to those who have their act sufficiently together to take advantage of the available opportunities. One of the best ways we can think of to make yourself luckier is to assume absolute and total responsibility for your own future. Whether you want wealth, challenging work in an exciting field, or the chance to make a contribution to society, it's up to you to get there.

We have laid out a four-year plan (see the Master Plan in Appendix I) to help you become a blue-chip graduate. The Master Plan is neither sacred nor etched in stone. It is an example of the sort of comprehensive planning we're talking about. If you start managing your time and your life now, you will accomplish light years more than you ever thought possible.

LIFE-PLANNING WORKSHOP

A Life-Planning Workshop is based on the premise that you are responsible for your own future in every area of your life. Your future doesn't just happen. You create it. Of course, it's true that you have personal and historical limitations. Michael Jordan and Meryl Streep were endowed with natural talents that most of us can only dream about. It makes a difference whether you were born during an economic boom or a depression, during peacetime or war. And it's different being born into wealth and privilege than into poverty and oppression. Still, it's up to you to determine your future, regardless of the hand life has dealt you.

In a Life-Planning Workshop you might draw your own life line, from birth to death, and set the goals you want to accomplish before you die. You might fantasize a typical day in the kind of future you want for yourself. Or a special day. You might be asked to write a press release about yourself on your fortieth birthday. Or write your own obituary.

Attending a Life-Planning Workshop can be an interesting and stimulating way to make yourself a more effective, goal-directed person. Chances are that one of the student service agencies on your campus (see Chapter 10) offers such a workshop. If not, ask them to do so!

THE HIGH COST OF CHAOS

Mary Elizabeth had problems. Her office looked like a family of chimpanzees had rung in the New Year there. One good sneeze would start a paper avalanche. She glanced sadly around the room, eyeing the uneven stacks of reports, the jumble of records, the half-open file drawer overflowing with folders. Somewhere in the midst of all that clutter was her desk. She was faced with the unenviable task of cleaning it out.

Her career problems with the prestigious firm of Dynamic Testing had begun innocently enough. She had misplaced several test items that went with the new licensing exam. She should have had her secretary enter them onto the computer, but she'd been terribly busy the day the new items came in. By the time she found them and incorporated them into the exam, she was only ten days late. But the test editor didn't like the format. He said it was out of sequence. Revising the exam put Mary Elizabeth further behind schedule.

The printer attempted a rush job but didn't have the staff or equipment to speed things up. By the time the test distributor got the test, there was no hope of getting it to the testing sites on time. Sixteen centers nationwide were left with the costly task of rescheduling over thirty-five hundred people waiting to take their licensing exams.

Mary Elizabeth had always thought that her messiness was a sign of creativity. But now she realized it meant only that she was unemployed.

THE DOMINO THEORY

Hard to believe that so many people could be affected by one person's disorganization? Not really. In *The Organized Executive*, Stephanie Winston speculated that the Three Mile Island crisis could have been avoided if the manufacturers of the nuclear reactor had been more organized. The *New York Times*, on July 20, 1979, reported:

> Officials of the Babcock & Wilcox Company conceded
> that they had failed to take proper heed of warnings
> last year. They said the warnings, contained in memo-

randums written by assistants, had been sent to the wrong people, and had been subordinated to more pressing matters.

In other words, as Ms. Winston puts it, "the memorandums fell through the cracks."

Confusion at the start of a project can snowball into disaster. Because a few people at Three Mile Island didn't have their act together, tens of thousands of people had to suffer through a nightmare.

Granted, a messy desk doesn't usually lead to nuclear meltdown, but if you want a career in the big leagues, you've got to stay organized.

Nor do you have to wait till you graduate. Being an academic slob can cost you plenty long before you ever put on your cap and gown. Suppose you lose your notes for tomorrow's killer Organic Chemistry midterm. You search your room with a thoroughness and zeal that would make James Bond proud. But no notes. You retrace your steps. Each classroom. The library. Still no notes. And Professor Shaft's tests always come from his lectures. You call the one friend that's taking the same class. No answer. He might be in the study lounge. Or his girlfriend's apartment. Or the Chemistry Lab. Or . . . get the picture?

Most professionals have a well-organized office. They need one if they want to be productive enough to remain competitive. If you're serious about becoming a blue-chipper, you need one too.

GETTING STARTED

Find yourself a workspace. It's best to settle on one location and stick with it. Use it only for work. That way, everytime you're there, you'll know it's time to get down to business.

Your workspace should be as distraction-free as possible. It should have good lighting and a decent writing surface. It should feel good to you. If your room won't work, try a carrel in the library.

TURNING YOUR ROOM INTO A MINI-OFFICE

Choose a desk or table that is approximately twenty-eight inches high and wide enough to give you room to spread out. An uncomfortable height causes strain, which is distracting and means you learn less. Get a comfortable desk chair. Use it exclusively for study.

Select a lamp that doesn't waste desk space but still lights the desk. A lamp that attaches to the wall or side of the desk will leave more desktop workspace. Use lower wattage lightbulbs. More watts don't make better light, just brighter light that may be harsher. Experiment. Find the best lighting for you.

Storage for books and supplies is important. You don't want to have to go on a hunting expedition everytime you start to study for a different course. Bookcases, shelving, or, at the very least, bookends on the desktop can be used. An inexpensive desktop bookshelf can be made if you can't attach conventional shelves to the wall. Most lumber companies will cut wood for a minimum charge per cut.

The space under the shelf can be used to store smaller supplies; the remaining shelves can be used for books and larger supplies. Having your things readily available saves time and avoids disruption. If possible, buy extra supplies and store them either in the top of the closet or under the bed. It's usually cheaper to buy in bulk. A little forethought can save you the hassle of no typewriter ribbon the night before your term paper is due.

SETTING UP A FILE SYSTEM

Develop a file system—and use it. It will be easier to find what you need whenever you need it, not to mention eliminating tons of paper from your notebook.

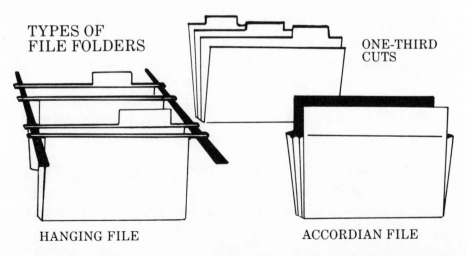

TYPES OF
FILE FOLDERS

ONE-THIRD
CUTS

HANGING FILE

ACCORDIAN FILE

OPTIONS FOR FILE STORAGE

File Cabinets: You can find inexpensive ones at office surplus stores, flea markets, used or discount furniture stores. Opt for letter-size storage capacity.

Heavy Corrugated Boxes: Find them at supermarkets, retail stores. Get one that will hold 8½D by 11D folders without too much excess space. A box that has been coated in wax (used in transporting perishable food items) or one that held heavy items (small TVs, radios) is more durable. Cover with self-adhesive decorative paper to make more attractive.

Milk Crates: Called stacking or storage cubes when sold at stores. Most are moderately priced. Dairies sell milk crates for as little as $2. Provide easy access for files; some have ridges at top to allow for hanging file folders.

File Boxes: More expensive and stronger ones are metal. Less expensive ones are soft plastic. Hinges may work out of plastic with frequent use. Both come in letter-size and have hinged lids. You can find them at office supply, retail, or discount stores.

After you've gotten a file container, you need to organize it. In categorizing, be as descriptive as possible without being too detailed. For example, instead of having a file on the library's hours and services, make a "College" file. If that is too broad, get more specific with "College, Services Available."

Suggested File Categories:
CURRENT COURSE WORK: tests, research notes, class notes, lab assignments, etc.
PAST COURSE WORK: tests, papers, projects. By subject.
SCHOOL: tuition, services, campus maps, advisors, etc.
MEDICAL: blood type, family physician, campus health insurance, diet, etc.
HOUSING: meal plans, utility bills, landlord, lease, etc.
WORK: taxes, benefits, insurance, appraisal ratings, job descriptions, etc.
EXTRACURRICULAR ACTIVITIES: organizations, officers, by-

laws, meeting times, activities planned, committee work, etc.

JOB SEARCH: potential employers, resumes, references and contacts, job search literature, etc.

TRANSPORTATION: car repair bills, maintenance schedule, insurance, license tag receipts, bus schedules, etc.

FINANCIAL: checking and/or savings accounts, bank statements, tax records, etc.

Subdivide files that have lots of information on many different subjects. One way to do this is by using separate file folders for each subdivision; then organize them in an accordion or hanging file. Another way is to subdivide a standard file folder by using page indexes.

Equipment Needed:

File Container: See insert on Storage Options.

File Folders: Letter-size. One-third cuts have higher visibility because of staggered tabs.

Accordion Files: Also called expandable folders.

Hanging Files: Require special hardware to use.

Bold Pens or Markers: Create high visibility.

Labels: If you really want to get fancy, try color-coding individual categories for instant recognition.

Even with an organized filing system, you may find yourself swimming in a sea of cellulose. Naturally, you want easy access to important papers without having to sort through useless garbage. Here are some ideas to get you started.

1. Handle each piece of paper once. Use it, file it, or trash it.

2. When in doubt, throw it out.

3. Keep a folder for each current course. Subdivide it into categories, such as TESTS, CLASS NOTES, RESEARCH PAPERS, HOMEWORK ASSIGNMENTS, and LAB WORK. Store these in the front of your file box where they can be easily reached. File all relevant papers the day you get them. (Hint: As you file,

review each page. This will reinforce what you learned that day.)

4. Keep a folder for past courses that are related to your major or minor. When a class is no longer current, weed out useless or repetitive material. Remove the dividers and staple the contents together. Put all related material into one folder. For example, Abnormal Psychology, Social Psychology, and The Psychology of the Terminally Gross and Disgusting could easily be stored in one folder labeled Psychology. File alphabetically.

5. If you have a glut of elective course material on the same subject, put it together. If it covers a wide variety of subjects, file several in one folder. Label it descriptively. For example, Electives: Fish Management, Temperate Zone Fruit Crops, The Movies as Narrative Art. If it isn't worth saving, donate it to a "Save the Trees" campaign.

QUICK SCORING ORGANIZATION QUIZ

Points   Score

1. 0   I have no address book.
    1   I have an address book in my dorm or apartment.
    2   I have an address book in my purse or wallet.
    3   I have the address and telephone number of my   *3*
        family physician in my address book.   _____

2. 0   I have no appointment calendar.
    1   I have an appointment calendar in my dorm or
        apartment.
    2   I carry an appointment calendar with me.
    3   My appointment calendar has important dates from   *2*
        my class syllabi marked.   _____

3. 0   I have no place to keep important papers such as old
        tests, research papers, medical records . . .
    1   I keep important papers together, but in no particu-
        lar order.
    2   I have an organized filing system.
    3   I keep a separate folder for each current class that is
        subdivided by categories such as tests, research   *1*
        papers, class notes.   _____

4. 0   I have no place where I regularly study.
    1   I have a place of study which has adequate lighting,
        little to no noise, a comfortable writing surface,
        and easy access to office supplies such as pens,
        pencil sharpener, etc.
    2   I have a place of study which is within easy access to
        my filing system.
    3   My place of study has ALL of the following items: *3*
        dictionary, thesaurus, and style manual.   _____

5. 0   I don't know where the main library is.
    1   I know where the reference department in the main
        library is.
    2   I know where the *Reader's Guide to Periodical Lit-*
        erature is.   *3*
    3   I know how to use it.   _____

Scoring:

0	Points —	Evidence indicates you may not be alive and/or enrolled at an institution of higher learning. Time to get your act together.
1-5	Points —	A faint resemblance to a blue-chip student can be seen. Since strong organizational skills are critical to a blue-chipper, I wouldn't pick out a BMW just yet.
6-10	Points —	The smell of success is in the air. You are on your way to becoming a blue-chipper. Pat yourself on the back.
11-15	Points —	Real blue-chip material. IBM's spies have probably already spotted you and sent your name to their recruiters.

SUMMARY

1. Successful businesses are organized. So are blue-chip graduates.
2. Set goals and determine the activities that will help you reach those goals.
3. Plan your time for the quarter or semester.
4. Establish weekly and daily schedules.
5. Prioritize every day.
6. Set up a work space.
7. Develop a file system.
8. Keep class material organized.

4
Making
The Grade(s)

You (or your parents) are forking over anywhere from $25,000 to $50,000 for a college education. Why not get your money's worth? A high GPA isn't 100 percent proof that you learned a lot, but it's an indicator. And grades will influence what kind of job offers you get when you graduate. They're not everything, but they're easily quantifiable and they do make a difference.

WHY GRADES ARE IMPORTANT

Whether you're in engineering, journalism, or accounting, grades are considered a direct measure of your technical expertise. Boeing doesn't want somebody who barely squeezed by in design class developing their airplanes. You can make up for low grades with superior performance in other areas, particularly if you plan to go into sales. But most Fortune 500 corporations hire new accountants and management trainees who have solid academic records. A recruiter for IBM assures us that the majority of the new people they hire are the academic cream of the crop. So who wants to work for IBM? Very possibly you! They pay well and have a reputation for treating their employees fairly and honestly.

If you want to be a physician or a lawyer, you've got to have good grades. Otherwise, no medical school, no law school. And it's the same if you want a career in science—without the grades you'll never get into graduate school (see Appendix V). So keep your options open. Make a real effort in your classes. Given the current debate about the quality of American education, we predict that the academic records of most graduates will be more closely scrutinized in the future. And that includes prospective public school teachers.

Suppose your roommate graduates with a 3.7 compared to your 2.4. If his best job offer is for $2,000 more than yours, even if he performs no more effectively than you throughout his career, that $2,000 difference may well remain. Over a thirty-year career that adds up to $60,000. If you figure that raises are often determined as a percentage of salary, that adds up to more dollars. And if he should invest his extra money wisely (and he probably will), his nest egg will grow still bigger. It doesn't take much of a head start to add up to a gap of a quarter-million dollars over the long haul.

But, you say, money isn't everything. What about location, the challenge of a particular job, doing something you really like? The same principle applies: the better your collegiate performance, the more choices you'll have.

AIM FOR THE TOP

Imagine for a moment that you're an outstanding tennis player. Your burning ambition is to be a top pro. To that end you've signed up for four extended instructional camps. It will cost you plenty of green, but you're convinced it will eventually pay off. This camp has top-flight instructors and outstanding facilities. There's a library of instructional films. There are grass, clay, and hard surface courts. There are other players to hit against, ball machines to perfect your strokes on, strategy sessions conducted by Jimmy Connors and Martina Navratilova. You get the picture.

Most novice athletes would drool over this kind of a chance. Yet, when you get to camp, you discover that some of the campers couldn't care less about being there. They spend most of their time playing video games or cards. They watch endless *M*A*S*H* reruns on the tube. Some get drunk every other night. They don't get enough sleep, and they don't eat right. They avoid the drills that would enable them to perfect their strokes because drills are too boring for them. When they play matches, they play against only the weaker players so they can be sure of winning. They leave the first camp in not much better shape than when they started it. Between camps they don't practice at all. They enter a few minor tournaments and don't do well in those. And this goes on for four years.

Crazy, right? They'll never make it to Wimbledon. Yet this is a pretty good description of how a lot of students waste four years of college. Their chances of success are no better.

But wait a minute. Most students don't lead lives of total dissipation during their college years. *Animal House* was an entertaining movie, but it was fiction.

We'd have to agree with you. The typical college student is neither as funny nor as self-destructive as the character portrayed by John Belushi. But then the average undergraduate is not on the high road to success, either.

To go back to our tennis analogy, most students do go to a fair number of their classes. Most practice their strokes from time to time. And that's about it. They might make it past the first or second round in a typical tournament, but they rarely get any further. They're never going to make it to the big leagues either. Wimbledon will remain just a fantasy.

That's the way it is with most college students. (Remember Sam Dresden?) They get by. They don't cause anybody all that much trouble. But they're not really going anywhere. When they graduate, they'll have to settle for leftovers. If you want better than second-rate, you need a competitive edge. You need to know how to be a blue-chip student before you can be a blue-chip graduate.

BLUE-CHIP STUDY SKILLS
Reading

You may have been raised on Captain Kangeroo and Pac Man, but you will probably spend a good deal of your professional life reading. Reading reports, memos, proposals, business letters. Reading research and background material to keep up in your field. Besides, reading is an integral part of any intelligent person's entire life. It helps you become an informed citizen of the world you live in. It's an unlimited means of personal enrichment and pleasure. Obviously, reading well—rapidly, with comprehension and retention—is a big advantage.

Reading is an integral part of your life, not just something comparative literature majors need to be good at. But if reading well is important in the corporate world, it is absolutely essential in college. We've worked with students for years and have found this to be true even among science and engineering students.

If you do not read well, we recommend getting some basic assistance from your campus Learning Resource Center. In some schools reading effectiveness is taught by the English department. We won't guarantee that you'll be able to read *War and Peace* in five minutes, but that sort of speed isn't really relevant for your collegiate reading.

How do you know you need assistance with your reading? A low verbal score on the SAT is one indicator. A distaste, bordering on loathing, for reading is another. Poor grades in history and literature can be a tip-off. Probably the clearest sign that you don't read well is the fact that you struggle daily with reading your textbooks. Or at least whenever you try to study one. You may have the experience of reading and rereading several pages without remembering what you've just covered.

Because reading and understanding textbooks is so crucial to being a blue-chip student, we will focus our attention on helping you do it better. Be advised that there are other forms of reading that will be required of you during your career. But if you can handle your textbooks, you've got a leg up as far as college goes.

Studying Textbooks

There are three steps to studying a textbook: 1. Preview; 2. Read; 3. Review. Each is essential if you want to maintain maximum efficiency.

PREVIEWING: Failure to preview a chapter before actually reading it is probably the most common error that students make. Without previewing material you don't give your mind the chance to establish categories for storing the information you're about to receive. A good public speaker first tells you what he's going to say, then he says it, then he tells you what he said. Previewing gets you ready for what's going to come so that you can catch it, digest it, and store it. If you're ready for it, your mind will tend to wander less from the subject, and you'll soak up more. No more reading the same page five times without remembering what it is that you've just read.

We recommend three previewing steps:
  a. read the introduction, the summary, and any study questions;
  b. read the headings, the captions, anything in boldface;
  c. read the first sentence of each paragraph.

This has taken you only a few minutes, and you already have a good overview of the chapter. (As a budding blue-chipper with growing organization skills, you're not likely to fall behind in your classes very often. But if you do and you have very little time to study for a test, your best bet is simply to preview all the material to be covered. You may retain enough to pass the test.)

READING: You're familiar with the chapter. You know what to expect from it. Now you're ready to read it.

We recommend three reading steps:
  a. Read the chapter through from beginning to end. Don't underline anything yet or make any notes;
  b. Now, go back and underline or highlight what you've just read;
  c. Distill the key point into your own words in the margin or onto a study sheet.

Because you previewed the chapter before you actually read it, your reading has been more effective than ever before. Because you read and understood the material before you underlined it or made any notes, you will have underlined only the important concepts and facts. Your notes will be pertinent. You will also discover that this sort of active reading forces you to learn the material. This chapter is now yours. You will probably never have to read it word for word again. Instead, you have a manageable amount of material to study the night before the test: what you've underlined and your notes.

REVIEWING: Professional musicians still practice their scales. Professional tennis players have to practice their strokes. And you have to review. This is because of a phenomenon called the Curve of Forgetting.

You start forgetting as soon as you stop learning. One psychologist found that in only twenty minutes he forgot about half of the nonsense syllables he had memorized. In another experiment students forgot almost half of the textbook material they had learned within twenty-four hours.

The solution to this universal student problem comes in two parts. First, you retain what you understand much better than what you simply commit to rote memory. So do your level best to grasp the underlying principles of each subject. Try to fit the facts into the overall scheme of things. Second, you must practice regular review. If you have read your textbooks the way we have suggested, you have already distilled what you need to know down to a manageable level. Now, review it regularly.

An especially powerful way to improve retention of material is to recite it. Often. Oral recitation is effective because it allows you to check whether you really know the material or not. It's one thing to be able to recognize something as familiar. It's quite another to be able to recall it and state it on your own. Since you speak much more slowly than you think, you also give your brain the necessary time to

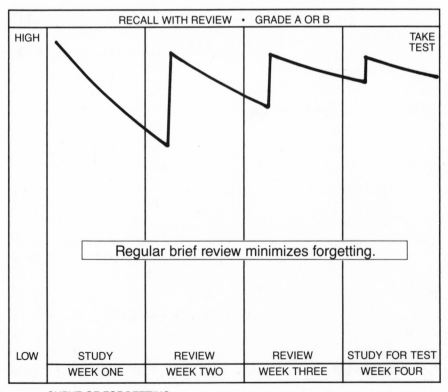

CURVE OF FORGETTING

establish firm memory traces.

Students often confuse reading their textbooks with studying. Nothing could be further from the truth. Reading something just once means you'll forget most of it. Reading it several times takes too long. An effective reading system prepares you to review. *Reviewing is studying*. So review. Often.

Come test time, no more all-nighters. No cramming. No last minute confusion and panic. All you do is study what you've underlined and your notes, get a good night's sleep—and knock the top off the test curve. Being a blue-chip student can be kind of fun.

Improve Your General Reading Ability

Did you know that top executives generally have very large vocabularies? If you're aiming for upper-level management, a "Dick, Jane, and Spot" level of reading comprehension is a definite handicap. One way to improve your vocabulary is by reading with a dictionary at

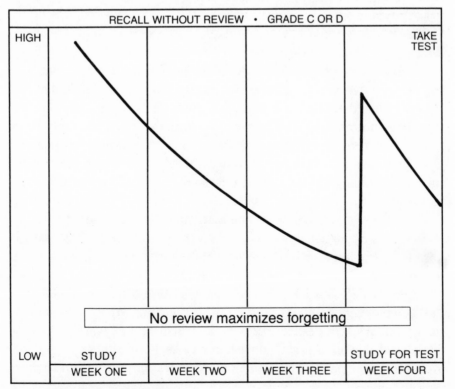

CURVE OF FORGETTING

hand. Of course, this works only if you use the dictionary.

We recommend reading a variety of material. An occasional trashy novel ups your speed. More literary fare increases your vocabulary. And also, we believe, your wisdom. Read the newspaper. Read a weekly newsmagazine. Read the *Wall Street Journal*. Read *Esquire* sometimes or *Fortune* or *Savvy*. Try *Harper's* or the *Atlantic*. Take a look sometimes at professional magazines and find out what's happening in your field. We have found that reading the weekly *New York Times Book Review* section is one of the most efficient ways to keep up with new ideas and trends. This is the Information Age. If you expect to keep up with it, you'd better read.

Learning in Class

The same principles that help you conquer that thrilling pageturner, *Economics in Theory and Practice*, by James Johnson, can help you soak up knowledge like a sponge in class: 1. Prepare; 2. Observe and Record; 3. Review.

Let's take each principle in turn.

PREPARING: You have to be ready if you expect to be effective. We suggest three components:

(a) Have a tough, no-nonsense attitude. We don't mean that you should take every word uttered by your professors as infallible. Far from it. Just don't feel too sorry for yourself because your biology teacher is not as easy to follow as Mr. Rogers. You'll probably have some great professors and some who aren't so hot. Just remember, you don't have to like teachers to learn from them. Figure that your tuition is helping to pay your professors' salaries. Try to get your money's worth;

(b) Review your notes from the last time the class met;

(c) Read any material in the textbook that is related to what will be covered in the lecture. Be ready with questions on anything you don't understand.

OBSERVING and RECORDING: Sit front and center. In general, the highest grades come from the first three rows. We know it sounds corny, but it's true. Sociologists E. J. Walsh and Howard Schuman discovered this bit of practical wisdom in a series of studies conducted over a ten-year period. Maybe it's because it's harder for you to doze off with Professor Long hovering over you. At least you can hear what he's saying. Maybe it's because he thinks your enthusiasm for Renaissance literature earns you the benefit of the doubt come grade time. Probably it's because you'll learn more in spite of yourself when you sit at your professors' feet than when you sit on the back row of a large lecture hall, staring out the window, contemplating the pain of unrequited love. And the more you learn, the more fun college becomes. Or at least it's more tolerable.

Sit upright and breathe deeply. No, we are neither your mother nor the Marines. It's just that decent posture improves your breathing, which maintains the proper level of oxygen in your bloodstream, which feeds your brain, which keeps you awake and alert. Participate. Ask questions if you don't understand. Volunteer for demonstrations. Take risks.

And take good notes.

Obviously, taking good notes requires your classroom attendance, but it's worth the effort. Another finding of the Walsh/Schuman studies is that students who make the best grades attend class more often than those with poorer grades.

Experiment with the Cornell Method or with Mind Mapping.

In the Cornell Method you make a vertical line about three inches from the left edge of each sheet of paper. You take notes from the lecture to the right of that line. The left side of the line is reserved for key words and concepts that organize the material on the right. You can then use the keys in this column as flash cards when you review. See if you can recite the points on the right by looking at the concepts on the left.

In Mind Mapping you begin in the middle of the page with the main point and jot down subsidiary points on the rest of the page. Eventually you connect the points with lines and arrows and add sub-points.

(Our example of Mind Mapping comes from our work in preparing this book. The example of the Cornell Method is typical of notes you might take in your English composition class.)

REVIEWING: Clarify and organize your notes as soon as you can. Stay a few minutes after class and do it then, if possible. Definitely bring order to your notes before you go to sleep. Then review your notes periodically. The Forgetting Curve applies to lecture notes the same as to textbook material.

CORNELL METHOD

	English Comp
Purposes of c/c writing	Comparison — how things are similar
	Contrast — how they are different
	Discussing 2 items together =
	better understanding of both
Divided or block method	Discuss everything about item A, then
	everything about item B; easier for writer,
	harder for reader; sometimes forget or
	lose sight of thesis; works best on short
	pieces
Alternating or point-by-point method	Discuss first point for A & B, then move to
	second point for A & B, and so on; harder
	for writer, easier for reader; forces
	stronger thesis and sharper organization;
	works better on longer pieces
Teacher's preference	Probably best to use alternating method
	for most assignments
Similarities to other kinds of writing	Always need strong argumentative thesis;
	lots of specific details to support main
	points; make sure points are in best order
	to support thesis; keep organizing
	principle clear

MIND MAPPING

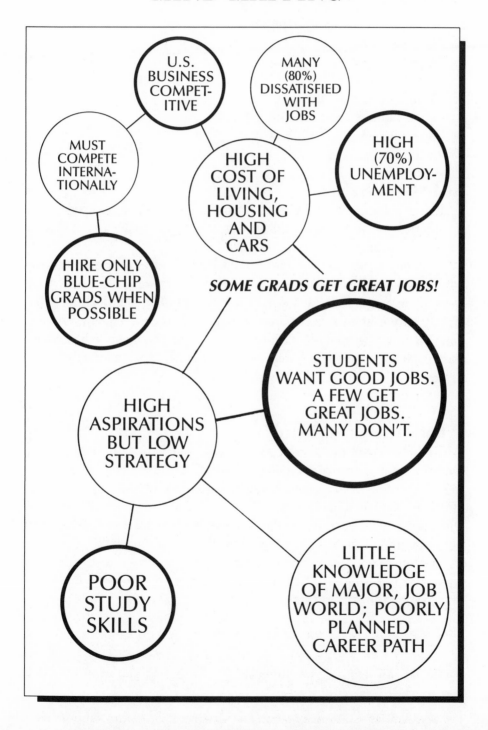

Seven Tips On Taking Effective Notes

1. Develop your own abbreviations.
2. Write concepts in your own words.
3. Write key terms in prof's words.
4. Copy from board.
5. Use only one side of paper.
6. Label, number, and date all notes.
7. Use white space. Don't crowd.

ACING TESTS

Taking tests is the easy part if you have gotten organized. The techniques we have suggested for digesting your textbooks and lectures are nothing more than organized study.

Think of yourself as the Chief Executive Officer of your own knowledge business. Grades are an index of your earnings. Naturally, you want to manage your business to show a profit. You work as efficiently as possible because time is money. And so is energy, so you don't want any wasted effort. Even if you're not the most dedicated or the brightest student in your class, studying systematically gets better results than studying haphazardly.

What's the Good Word?

Try to look over old tests if you can get your hands on them. Some fraternities and sororities maintain test files affectionately referred to as "The Word." Some schools require the library to keep copies of old tests so that non-Greeks will not be at an unfair disadvantage. One good use for such tests is to consider them a practice test. We do not recommend that you limit your study to the old tests.

As soon as you know when a prof is going to give a test, ask him what sort of test it will be and what material will be covered. Don't prepare for the wrong test!

OK, so you've studied systematically. Naturally, you want to maximize your results on the actual tests themselves.

Hints For Taking *Any* Test

1. Be on the offensive. Think of a test as an opportunity to show your professor how much you know.
2. Show up on time or a few minutes early. Be sure to have all necessary equipment (pencils, pens, bluebooks, etc.) at hand. You don't want to start your test harried and flustered. Arrive comfortable. Don't come in hungry, thirsty, or wearing clothes that bind or shoes that pinch.
3. Scan the entire test. Attack the test according to the value of each question, problem, or section. Devote 50 percent of your time to the part of the test that's worth 50 percent of the credit. Don't waste twenty minutes on a question worth only two points.
4. Read each question slowly and carefully. Then reread it. You won't get much credit for a great answer to a question your professor didn't ask. Ask the teacher to explain any question you find unclear.
5. Answer the easy questions first. Then work on those that are more difficult or less familiar.
6. Check your answers. If you have time, check them again. You don't get bonus points for finishing early and being the first to leave the room.

Guidelines For Essay Tests

1. Pay careful attention to the directions in the questions. Make sure you really do "compare and contrast" or "explain" if that is what is asked of you.
2. Think through your answer first. Outline it on scratch paper before you start writing your final answer.
3. Support your answer with facts.
4. Review each answer. Your grade will be based on what you actually wrote, not on what you intended to write.
5. Leave space between your answers so you can add to them if you recall forgotten material later on.
6. Put something down for each question. Partial credit is better than no credit at all.

7. If you run out of time before you have finished the test, quickly jot down outlines for answers to remaining questions.

Suggestions For Problems Tests

1. Jot down hard-to-remember formulas as soon as the test is in hand. (If you do this before the test is distributed, you might be accused of cheating.)
2. Don't get hung up on a difficult problem. Come back to it after you have finished others you can do more easily.
3. Show each step. Box and label your answer.
4. Check your solutions if you have time. If possible, use different steps. For example, add up instead of down. It's very easy to make arithmetic or algebraic errors.
5. Even if you know your answer is wrong, turn it in. You might get partial credit for taking some of the right steps.

Tips For Objective Tests

1. Read each question carefully. Read it like a lawyer.
2. Watch out for negatives and double negatives and qualifers. One word can change the meaning of a statement from true to false.
3. Unless specifically told that wrong answers bring an extra penalty, guess if you don't know.
4. Watch out for tense, number, and gender. The right answer should agree on all counts.

Getting Your Test Back

One of the keys to being a blue-chip student is learning *from* your tests as well as for them. You may be tempted to toss a test, especially if you did poorly on it. Don't do it! Carefully review every returned test. Find out where you went wrong, and make up for any gaps in your knowledge. Get help from a friend or the professor if you need to. File every test for review before the final exam.

USING THE LIBRARY

Living in the Information Era (see Chapter 5) means expertise will probably be a job candidate's most marketable asset. And expertise today has a bewilderingly short half-life. John Naisbitt, in *Megatrends*, notes that scientific and technical information now doubles in less than six years. He predicts that before long it will double in less than two years. The future belongs to those who can keep up with this mushrooming amount of knowledge.

As we have suggested throughout this chapter, you can own a piece of the future by developing basic intellectual and learning skills. Reading, writing, and mathematical reasoning are the foundations. Next come computer literacy and mastery of the library. Increasingly, these two go together.

Knowing how to research the causes of World War I effectively doesn't enable you just to write a good history paper. It means you'll also know how to investigate a field of study when you choose a major. It means you'll know how to find out about a corporation or agency when you go job hunting in a few years. It means that you'll be able to keep up with the twenty-first century throughout your life.

A necessary step in staying informed in your field is to read a respected professional journal regularly. If you're really serious, the best way to keep up is to read a book of abstracts in your field.

Even the library at the smallest school has more books than you would ever read in a lifetime. So how do you find the right book? Or how do you find out if your library has information on a particular topic?

You probably already know how to use the card catalog or the microfiche system employed by larger libraries. Every book in the library is listed in the card catalog by: 1. Author; 2. Title; 3. Subject.

If you don't know the author or title, try the subject index. Broad areas, such as biology, electrical engineering, or journalism, will be subdivided to help you find more specific topics. For example:

BIOLOGY—Dictionaries

BIOLOGY—Methodology

BIOLOGY—Study and Teaching.

Many of your library's holdings are in circulation. You can check them out of the building. There is also a goldmine of reference material that stays. You should know about it as well. Our "Guide to

QUICK GUIDE TO REFERENCE MATERIAL	
PERIODICAL NAME	**SUBJECT INDEXED**
Reader's Guide to Periodical Literature	Popular Magazines
Index Medicus	Medicine
Psychological Abstracts	Psychology
Education Index	Education
Public Affairs Information Service (PAIS) Bulletin	Economics & Politics
Modern Language Association (MLA) International Bibliography	Modern Languages
Social Science Index	Social Sciences
Humanities Index	Humanities
Business Periodicals Index	Business and Company Information
The New York Times Index	News & Current Events
The Wall Street Journal Index	Business and Financial Information
Applied Science and Technology Index	Practical Science and Engineering

Reference Material" is by no means exhaustive.

If you have problems finding something, *ask a librarian.* Remember, they're working for you. Make sure you get your money's worth. This doesn't mean you should expect them to do your research for you, but they can and will help you get started. And they probably know about sources of information you haven't even dreamed of.

Most colleges offer courses on using the library. Consider taking one. One of the main differences between high school and college is that you'll have to read much more material in college and write many more papers. If you master the library early on, you will save yourself countless hours. You will also be able to come up with facts and sources that impress your professors.

Make your life as a student easier. Make yourself more competitive. Know how to use the library.

WRITING PAPERS

Most professional jobs require writing skills. You don't necessarily have to be a Shakespeare or even a Stephen King, but the ability to write a clear, convincing proposal and a concise, readable report will raise your stock in just about any company. Ironically, being a professional writer is not a high-paying job. But writing well in combination with other skills can only add to your blue-chip stock. It also makes college easier and means higher grades.

Some suggestions: If you have a choice of topics, pick one that interests you. The better your motivation, the less painful the task. You will probably also write a better paper. Sometimes it's helpful to pick a topic that will increase your expertise in an area relevant to your career. This may be difficult your freshman year. Knowing the causes of the Civil War isn't usually a particularly marketable chunk of information. But as you get into your upper-level courses, it will pay you to research something that will someday make you a better engineer, accountant, or city planner.

We know of graduate students who made it a point to write every term paper in such a way that it could also be published in a professional journal. By the time they graduated, they had string of publications that increased their blue-chip status. This is a good strategy for undergraduate journalism and advertising majors also.

A word of caution here. Don't be practical all the time. We say go after a topic sometimes just because you're curious about it. How else will you get a larger view of the world? You're not going to have only a career after you graduate. You're also going to be a citizen, a friend, a lover, and probably a parent.

And also, we hope, a well-rounded human being.

The first steps in writing a good paper are managing your time efficiently and collecting good information. These are the same steps that you can some day use to write a winning proposal. Start with the date the paper is due, and work backwards from there. If a major paper is due on Friday, November 16, you want it finished a day or so before. That means the final editing and proofreading should occur on Wednesday or Thursday. You write the paper a few days before that. And so on, back to your research of the topic.

Suppose on October 1 you are assigned a major paper to be turned in on November 16. You would schedule something resembling the following deadlines:

1. 10/1-10 Research general area to find interesting and/or professionally enhancing topic;
2. 10/11-28 Research topic. Duplicate key articles. Check out key
   books;
3. 10/29-11/5 Take notes, preferably on index cards;
4. 11/6 Make out bibliography on index cards;
5. 11/7 Organize notes and outline paper;
6. 11/8-9 Write body of paper;
7. 11/10 Write introduction & conclusion. Title it;
8. 11/12 Reread and edit, first for content, then for style;
9. 11/13 Type it;
10. 11/14 Proofread and correct errors;
11. 11/15 Take in a movie while your roommate is embarking on a
    migraine producing all-nighter to finish his paper.

"You're crazy," you might be thinking. "I'd never want to work that hard for that long on one lousy paper." But wait a minute! What we're recommending is actually the *easy* way. Remember, it's your room-mate who gets the headaches. And probably the bad grade. You, on the other hand, work at a leisurely pace with minimum strain and maximum results. All we can say is, "Have you tried it?" Once you do, we predict you'll be a convert. And you'll also be preparing yourself to hit the floor running when you land that first blue-chip job after graduation.

A few more words about steps 3, 4, and 5. By entering each reference on an index card, you can easily arrange them alphabetically and type out your bibliography. Similarly, by keeping your notes on cards, you will be able to arrange them in a "tree" or pyramid (see insert). From there, it is easy to develop a tight, logical outline.

INDEX CARD PYRAMID

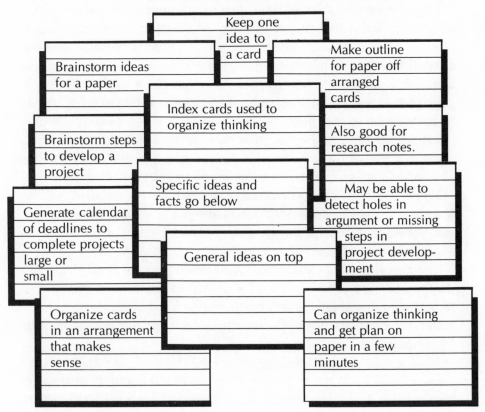

TAKING ADVANTAGE OF YOUR PROFESSORS

You read the heading right. We don't mean taking "unfair" advantage. We don't recommend that you try to deceive or manipulate your professors. Nor should you try to get them to do what you can do for yourself. But don't forget: your tuition helps pay their salary. They're working for you just as much as you're working for them. Get your money's worth.

Too many students look at the relationship between students and faculty as adversarial—it's us against them. Professors are the barrier between me and a degree and a good job. We think a much healthier outlook is to view your teachers as your consultants and guides.

You're investing a lot of time, money, and energy in your college education. You'd like to get established on your career path, gain some general knowledge about the world, and acquire some wisdom as well. The more help you can get from your professors on all counts, the farther along you'll be. Granted, the expertise and commitment of your professors will vary considerably. Some are burdened with too many classes. Many have enormous workloads—research, administration, writing, and committee meetings all distract them from classroom preparation. You want them to help you get ready for the real world, but you've got to be insistent to get their attention.

When you take tennis lessons, you wouldn't be satisfied with a teacher who never drilled you or made you practice. Why pay for instruction that doesn't improve your game? Does it make sense to expect any less of your professors?

The problem is not that your profs work you too hard, but that they're too busy to teach you all you need to know. So pester them. Ask them questions. Participate in class. Visit them during office hours to pick their brains. Be assertive. Insist on getting all you can from them.

Most of your professors chose college teaching because they love it. Show a little enthusiasm for learning, and they'll almost always be cooperative. And when you discover which faculty members on your campus are particularly dedicated and talented, sign up for every one of their courses that you can.

SUMMARY

1. A college education is expensive. Get your money's worth.
2. Better grades get better jobs. You *must* have good grades to get into graduate school.
3. Reading and writing well make college easier and prepare you for professional work.
4. The three main steps in studying a textbook are: Preview, Read, and Review.
5. The three main steps to learning in class are: Prepare, Record, and Review.
6. Use a systematic method of note-taking such as the Cornell Method or Mind Mapping.
7. Be familiar with the different types of tests and prepare accordingly.
8. We live in the Information Age: You'll have to keep learning throughout your life if you want to stay current and marketable.
9. Master the library.
10. Develop a series of deadlines on your calendar for every major paper or project.

5
Doctor, Lawyer, Chief Executive Officer

Lots of people don't like their jobs. In Chapter 1 we cited career expert, Tom Jackson, who states that 80 percent of the American work force are dissatisfied with their jobs. Richard Bolles, author of the perennial best seller *What Color Is Your Parachute?*, estimates that one-third of all job hunters are looking while still employed. In other words, their dissatisfaction is strong enough to press them into action. You don't want to join the ranks of the chronically dissatisfied. You want something better.

You can have a satisfying career, but it's not going to happen by accident. It takes a hard, honest look at yourself and an active search of the job world.

It amazes us that so many students skimp here. After graduation, you can count on spending as many as ten thousand days at the office. Nearly half of your adult waking hours will be spent working. Doesn't it make sense to spend a little time now to get it right?

THE COUNSELING CENTER

OK, we're probably a little biased, but we think it's almost imperative for you to get career counseling. The stakes are too high for you not to. And the cost is too low to pass it up. Almost every university and college has an agency that provides free vocational guidance. Use it. If you want to get the most out of your counselor and, later on, out of your career, there are some other things you can do, too. First, here are the services you can expect from a typical college counseling center:

1. *Individual counseling.* A professional will help you appraise your interests, abilities, and work-related values. He or she can suggest sources of career information, including key individuals to contact.
2. *Group counseling.* Same as above, but with group support. You also have the opportunity to learn about different fields from the other members of the group.
3. *Testing.* No test can tell you what to do with your life, but the right tests can suggest careers to investigate. There are vocational interest inventories, aptitude tests, and personality tests. Interest inventories such as the Strong/Campbell are quite reliable and valid. Basically, they tell you which occupational types you share key interests with. If you checked many of the same items that successfully employed accountants do, for example, accountancy is probably a good field for you to investigate. Aptitude tests we're less keen on. High-school grades tend to be better predictors of collegiate performance than test scores. And work experience related to a field is the best gauge of your future performance in that field. Personality tests give you feedback about such variables as how independent or aggressive or achievement-oriented you might be.
4. *Computer-based guidance.* By interacting with a computer program you can learn the steps it takes to make a solid career decision. We're familiar with a program from National Testing Service (the nice people who brought you the SAT) called SIGI, which stands for System of Interactive Guidance and Information. (Actually, we have the new "industrial-strength" system which is called SIGI Plus.) In several hours at a terminal you can find out what careers match your values and abilities, get information about those careers, find out what steps you should take to pursue a particular career, and actually make a simulated career choice that takes into account your possible job satisfaction and the likelihood you could succeed in a particular career. We think it's an excellent tool and recommend it often to our students.
5. *Occupational Information.* Most centers have a library of career-

related material. A good book to start with is *The Occupational Outlook Handbook*, put out by the U.S. Department of Labor. Then go on to other printed literature, video cassettes, film strips, and any data banks on computer file. The more you know about a field, the easier it is to determine if it really suits you.

CRYSTALLIZING A VOCATIONAL IDENTITY

Maybe you're not actually enrolled in a college yet and don't have access to career counseling. Not to worry. There are many constructive steps you can take to help you to identify career goals.

College Catalog as Career Counselor

Go through your school's catalog and read the statement of purpose of each major division. (Divisions are usually called Schools or Colleges, as in "School of Business" or "College of Engineering.") Now, go back and read the statement of purpose of each department in each division that interested you. Next, identify and list the required courses that go with each department that intrigued you. Look up the course descriptions. Eliminate the departments with courses that don't appeal to you. Investigate further the departments with requirements that you think would interest and challenge you. Check out suggested elective courses. Talk with a departmental representative. Question some seniors who major in the department. Go to the campus book store and thumb through some introductory and advanced textbooks. By now, you will have narrowed down your list of departments to a more manageable number.

But don't stop now! Do some more research. How marketable is a particular major? What careers does it prepare you for? Find out. Read up on it. Check with Placement. Would I be good at it? (I might be interested in astronomy, but unless I'm a whiz at mathematics, I'd never make it through all the physics.) Take an introductory course. See if it matches your interests and abilities.

Vocational Navel Gazing Made Easy

There are about a zillion variations of the following exercise. We have cut it down to the bare bones minimum.

Take four sheets of paper. Draw a horizontal line across the middle of three of them. On the top half of the first, list those classes that you have liked or excelled in. On the second page, list preferred hobbies and activities. On the third, jot down any jobs you have held. What tasks did you perform in each job? List them. Now, on the bottom half of each page list the interests, values, and abilities suggested by the classes, activities, and tasks.

Now, look at the bottom half of each page for patterns and commonalities. Distill those common traits into a vocational self on the fourth page. The major you declare and the career you choose should be as compatible as possible with your vocational self.

The Real World

How many of you would agree to marry someone sight unseen? OK, it's a dumb question. Mail-order brides and arranged marriages belong to another time and place. You certainly wouldn't rely exclusively on gossip or propaganda about another person before you took the big plunge. You'd want some objective information. And you'd definitely want to spend some time with this person first.

We believe that choosing a career is at least as important as choosing a mate. Yet we find an incredible number of people who are willing to settle for mail-order majors or arranged careers. No wonder there's so much job dissatisfaction out there. The blue-chip graduate knows what he or she is getting into. And so should you.

Most majors acquaint you with a field. They don't necessarily prepare you for a job. Employers hire people to fill particular jobs. The more knowledgeable you are about jobs that match your needs and skills, the more likely you are to find the right one for you. You will also more likely convince an employer to hire you.

Just about the best way to find out about career opportunities is to get some career-related work experience before you graduate (see Chapter 6). Reading about something is never as revealing as trying it on for size. Besides, you can discover things like how a particular company treats its employees or how the different divisions of a corporation work.

Obviously you've got to have some inkling of a career goal before you can look for career-related work. But what if you're really up in the air about your future? What should you do then? And is there any general information about today's job world that you should know?

If you're thoroughly confused, get counseling. Also, do the College Catalog and the Voactional Navel Gazing exercises described above. As important as it is to know your vocational self, though, it is equally important to know something about the job world.

THE JOB WORLD

Find the Career Information Library on your campus. It's probably in the Counseling Center or at the Placement Office. If your college doesn't have a career library, you should be able to find plenty of information in the main library. Look over the *Occupational Outlook Handbook*. Check out any occupations that intrigue you. What sort of work is involved? What about pay and other benefits? What kind of training is required? Will you need additional degrees in order to advance? What does the future hold for the field? It's all in the *Handbook*, but don't stop there.

One of the best ways to find out about different kinds of work is through people who do the various jobs. Informational interviewing and networking are buzz words among professionals today and for good reason (see Chapters 8 and 15). You can learn about a career from professors and staff, from relatives and friends of the family, through your fraternity or sorority, at your church or temple, from alumni, and at your own job. All you need is the gumption to ask. And people like to talk about themselves, so most will be glad to discuss their work with you.

Conducting an Informational Interview

First, do your homework. Get an overview of the career you're investigating by reading up on it. It's presumptuous to expect a professional to teach you about his work when you haven't taken the trouble to learn a little about the basics. Besides, if you know something about a field, you can ask much better questions. More intelligent questions not only get better information, they also make you look good. There is no advantage to seeming like someone who just fell of the turnip truck.

But if you come across as a serious, thoughtful person who is genuinely interested in success, the person you're interviewing will probably not hesitate to recommend you to others in the field. They can provide you with additional information and may be the start of your network of professional contacts. (How about that? You thought you were simply finding out about a career, and you're already building a network!)

Another reason you want to make a good impression is that this person might be able to hire you for an internship next summer. Or give you a strong lead to someone else who might hire you or give you your first job after you graduate.

The other bit of homework you need to do before the interview is on yourself. Your contact will be able to give you more relevant information if he knows who he's talking to. We recommend developing a five-minute presentation. This is a short summary of your vocational interests, values, skills, and experiences. You give it early on in the interview, before you ask your questions.

Five-Minute Presentation of Janet Smith

Dr. Score, an industrial psychologist at Acme Enterprises, has just ushered Janet into his office. "So you think you might be interested in industrial psychology," he says. "What would you like to know?"

"A little bit of everything, but first I want to thank you for taking the time to talk with me. I'd also like to tell you a little about myself and how I got interested in the field, if it's all right with you. Dr. Schwartz said you could help me better if you knew a little about me."

Dr. Score smiles and nods for Janet to go on. She leans forward in her chair and begins.

"I'm a freshman at State U., and I'm majoring in psychology. I've always gotten along well with people—in school and band and church. But I've also been really curious about what makes people tick. I can remember watching *The Three Faces of Eve* one night on TV and being fascinated. After that I thought I wanted to be a psychiatrist. I read about Freud and Jung. I tried to figure out what my dreams meant and what everybody's hangups were.

"Then, my senior year I took a psychology course and learned that there was more to psychology than just being a therapist. And that a psychiatrist was a medical doctor, which I knew I didn't want to be. Also, our class took a field trip to a state mental hospital, and that seemed like a really depressing place to work. I thought some of the research that social psychologists did was very interesting. For a while I thought I might want to be a researcher, but I don't think I want to be in school that long."

"A lot of psychologists at the corporate level have PhDs," Dr. Score says. "And you pretty well have to have a master's to get started. The doctorate isn't as rigid a requirement as for clinicians though or if you want to teach at the college level."

"That's encouraging. It's not that I don't like college. It's just that I'm not sure I could afford to go to graduate school for very many years. Dr. Schwartz is trying to start up a graduate co-op program, and that could help me finance a master's degree if that's what I wind up doing."

"I think that's an excellent idea, but go on with what you were saying."

Janet, who was nervous about imposing on Dr. Score, is starting to feel more comfortable. He seems genuinely interested in helping her. She settles back in the chair and continues.

"We all had to take career tests in high school. I had interests in common with psychologists and social workers, but I also scored fairly high in a lot of the business careers. I'm in Dr. Schwartz's Intro class, and he told me Industrial/Organizational Psych might be a way for me to combine my interests and get into a branch of psychology that has a lot of opportunities.

"I made good grades in high school, and I made three *B*'s and an *A* my first quarter in college. I made just under 600 on both parts of my *SAT*. I'm pretty sure I'm going to make an *A* in Psych 301 this quarter. I don't consider myself a nerd, but I'm not afraid to work hard on my studies. I hope that gives you some idea about me. Can you tell me about your work here at Acme and how you got into organizational psychology?"

Listen attentively as your contact describes her field and what it's like to work in it. But do more than just listen. Obviously, it would be inappropriate to interrupt, but it's good form to interact. If some aspect of your contact's job particularly interests you, say so. Ask her for more details or how she feels about it. When you ask intelligent questions in a confident manner, you not only learn more, you are viewed as intelligent as well.

As you finish your interview, ask your contact if she can suggest other people who could give you useful information. Say your thank-you, and follow it up with a letter of thanks. Look over chapters 8, 13, and 15 to get more ideas on interviewing and networking.

THE JOB MARKET OF THE 90S AND BEYOND

Students often ask us which careers have the most promise. The answer, of course, is that no one knows for sure. The job market of the future depends on the interaction of the national and world economies, technological innovations, demographic changes, and a slew of other factors. Here are some educated guesses.

America Gets Middle-aged

The huge clump of the population born between 1947 and 1964 and known as the Baby Boom will be moving into middle age. Middle-aged people care about financial security—where they're going to retire and whether they'll be eating Alpo or lobster. Insurance and financial services will be important to middle-aged Baby Boomers. There will be a big demand for people to market and sell such services. And most of these positions will be relatively unaffected by international competition. Tony Lee, in the August 3, 1986 edition of the *National Business Employment Weekly,* predicts that accounting jobs will grow by 35 percent over the next ten years.

America Gets Old

More people will live longer. The Census Bureau projects that 12 percent of the population will be sixty-five or older by 1990. They will need geriatric services. There will be a big need for health-related workers. Yet, paradoxically, there will be much competition among health care facilities and providers. Medicine will be more of a business and will provide jobs for people in advertising, marketing, and management.

America Gets Educated

More people will be more highly educated. By 1995, 45 percent of the work force will be white-collar according to the 1986 Summer *Occupational Outlook Quarterly*. Less well educated people will be more susceptible to unemployment as the economy fluctuates. But with more college grads, there will be plenty of competition for professional jobs. The 1986 *Occupational Outlook Handbook* reported that, between 1970 and 1984, 20 percent of all college graduates were underemployed. Humanities majors in particular encountered employment problems. For this reason, fewer students are going into the humanities.

In our opinion this is unfortunate. An extensive study by AT&T showed that the liberal arts may be the *best* undergraduate preparation for management. This is because the humanities and social sciences provide an excellent education in verbal skills. Managers must be able to communicate well—both on paper and orally. The trouble is that too many anthropology and literature majors fail to develop a career focus and have no career-related work experience. We're convinced even philosophy majors can get good jobs if they follow the Blue-Chip Master Plan (see Appendix I).

Apparently more employers are beginning to see the wisdom of hiring graduates from the liberal arts. The Endicott Report of Northwestern University on college placement trends anticipated improved job prospects for such students in 1986. Also, CBS, Inc., has donated $750,000 to establish a corporate council on the liberal arts. Frank Stanton, a former CBS president with a degree in English, will direct research into how a liberal arts degree can help you in the business world.

Industrial Society Gives Way to the Information Era

Information will be America's number one product. Half of America's jobs have to do with information already. John Naisbitt in *Megatrends* predicts that the figure will be 70 percent within twenty years. By 1985 more people worked in universities than on farms. Many steel and auto workers were seriously suffering from unemployment. In the future, crops will still be grown, and goods will continue to be manufactured. But it will take fewer workers to produce either. Expertise will be highly marketable. Since expertise has a brief half-life in an era of high technology, knowing how to learn will be one of the most valuable skills you can acquire.

High Tech Will Get Higher

Scientific and technological jobs will be on the rise. The demand for different types of engineers varies with the supply of energy and with political decisions about national defense, space exploration, and environmental protection. As we write this chapter, chemical and petroleum engineers are having their troubles because of economic problems in the oil industry. The demand for electrical engineers, in particular, should keep on growing as should the need for mechanical engineers, systems analysts, and people who can work in the growing field of biotechnology. The 1986 Spring *Occupational Outlook Quarterly* predicts that scientists and engineers with management skills and training will be particularly hot properties.

FORTRAN Spoken Here

Computer literacy will be important for most professional level positions. Accountants will keep their books on computer files. Architects and illustrators will do much of their designing on computers. Managers will make many of their decisions with the aid of a computer spreadsheet. John Naisbitt compares computer illiteracy today with wandering around an enormous library in which all the books are randomly arranged. All that information, and no way to use it.

Can You Sell Doorknobs To Tent Dwellers?

People in sales will continue to have good opportunities, especially in growing industries. The 1986 Summer *Occupational Outlook Quarterly* predicts that jobs in sales will double by 1995. If you've got good persuasive skills, you can still make a bundle in sales, even if you're not a Phi Beta Kappa. High-paying sales areas—finance and insurance—will have more competition than jobs in retail sales.

So-So in the Social Sciences

The *Quarterly* for spring of 1986 estimates that jobs in the social sciences will experience faster-than-average growth. Competition for these jobs will be keen nonetheless because many students like to major in this area. Prospects are brighter for those with advanced degrees who go into applied areas. As we pointed out earlier, a successful business career is a distinct possibility for social science majors if they are focused and have career-related work experience. Don't forget the different outcomes for Sally Kowalski and Sam Dresden in Chapter 2.

Add on a Language

In spite of what our recruiter survey (see page 22) indicated, we'd be very surprised if knowledge of the right foreign language didn't turn out to be highly marketable. No, not Latin or Greek, but Chinese, Japanese, and Spanish will be highly useful in an increasingly international marketplace—if added on to an already marketable course of study.

We were talking recently with an economics student back from a year's internship in Japan. The student was convinced that the biggest barrier to increasing our exports to Japan was the simple fact that American products did not have clear Japanese instructions on them. He added that it was typical for American corporate representatives to show up at a Japanese trade show without even a rudimentary knowledge of the Japanese language and culture. This puts American businessmen at a tremendous disadvantage with their Japanese counterparts, most of whom do speak English. Small wonder there's a trade imbalance.

WHAT IF I'M STILL NOT SURE?

We're not surprised if you're a little uncertain. Life is filled with uncertainties. Some of you will be working twenty years from now in fields that haven't even been invented yet. If you want a 100 percent guarantee, you might consider inherited wealth. If you can't work that one out, and most of us can't, here are some other guidelines.

1. *Money isn't everything.* Sure, it's important, and you'd be a fool

to ignore your future financial security. But we're tired of talking to pre-meds who are more concerned with BMW's than Biochemistry. With engineering students who can't stand math and science, but figure they're going to ride the high-tech wave to megabucks. *Don't sentence yourself to a lifetime of work you're going to hate.*

A generation of psychological research on the work place has found that people were most satisfied when they were doing what they really wanted to do. Research by Tesesa Amabile of Brandeis suggests that they are most creative as well. After a certain level of income, salary and pats on the back have only a negligible impact on performance.

Besides, career choices are seldom limited to being a starving artist in Soho or a well-heeled financier on Wall Street. Why not be a creative director on Madison Avenue?

2. *There is no magic timetable.* Not even our Four-Year Master Plan. We're convinced it's a good general guide, but divine revelation it isn't. You don't *have* to declare a major by your sophomore year. And there's no crime in changing majors. The main thing is *don't just sit on your hands when it comes to choosing a major and planning your career.* Do the exercises and follow the suggestions in this chapter. Don't wander passively through college.

3. *There is no perfect career.* Nor does everyone "fall in love" with a career. True, some people are born doctors or lawyers or managers, but most aren't. Don't expect to hear angelic choirs every time you tackle a calculus problem just because you're majoring in physics.

There might be a dozen jobs out there that could meet your needs. Don't get tunnel vision and insist on one occupation and no other. What if you don't get into medical school? Or a good MBA program? Make sure you've got some decent alternatives in mind if everything doesn't go just as you planned it. Even blue-chippers have their setbacks. You'll probably have many jobs throughout your professional life. And you may well have more than one career.

SUMMARY

1. You're going to spend much of your adult life at work. Plan carefully how you're going to spend it.
2. Carefully assess your interests, abilities, and needs.
3. Thoroughly investigate relevant majors and careers.
4. Go to the source. Interview people who actually hold the job you think you might like.
5. Get help planning your career from whatever professional resources are available on your campus.
6. Getting career-related work before you graduate is one of the best ways to test your career choice.
7. No one can predict precisely what the future job world will be like. Therefore, general skills such as the ability to communicate, computer literacy, and the capacity to learn new information will help you to stay at the top.

6
Practice
Makes Perfect—
The Importance Of Work

You've been feeling rotten all day. The pain in your side has gotten progressively worse till you just can't stand it any longer. A friend drives you to the emergency room of the nearest hospital where your problem is diagnosed as acute appendicitis. You have to undergo an appendectomy immediately, and you can choose from three very bright physicians to perform the operation. One has read extensively about surgery in general and appendectomies in particular. He has never actually operated on anybody though. In fact, he has never even seen an appendectomy performed. The second doctor has read about such operations and he has seen them performed. The third has successfully performed an appendectomy several different times. Which doctor would you choose to open you up?

Most of us would choose the doctor who had the experience. Theory is great, but real-world practice counts for more on such an important task. Recruiters and employers feel much the same way about hiring someone to do a job for them. They want to know that you've done it before. If you have, you can probably do it again. This is why students who graduate on a co-operative plan tend to get better jobs. Their career-related work experience makes them better qualified candidates for the best jobs.

THE VALUE OF WORK

It's better to design circuits for McDonnell Douglas than to flip hamburgers for McDonald's. It's also better to manage for McDonald's than to push a broom at McDonnell Douglas. But any work is better than none at all. Working teaches you the importance of effort—employers appreciate and reward hard workers. Do you have to work nights and weekends to put yourself through school? (Approximately 50 percent of full-time college students worked during the 1985-1986 academic year.) It can be stressful, but you learn how to be self-sufficient. You also learn how to budget your time—you have no choice if you want to keep your grades respectable. Working teaches you responsibility, the importance of punctuality, how to get along with all kinds of people.

Employers like it when candidates have worked their way through school. We urge graduating seniors to highlight this fact on their resumes, even if they contributed only a portion of what their education cost them.

But career-related work is even better. What you learn is more relevant to your future, a fact that won't be overlooked by prospective employers when you graduate.

The right jobs while you're still in school will teach you about professional work. Co-ops and interns often work for corporations. They learn about a large company's different divisions. A nurse's aid might learn what it's like to work in a hospital or clinic. Even a file clerk can get a feel for how an office really operates. There will also be opportunities to make contacts—people who can write recommendations for you, give you leads for jobs, perhaps someday hire you for an important position.

One of the most valuable lessons you will learn is just where you fit into your chosen field. Or if you fit into it. Most college students change majors at least once. Better to find out as a rising sophomore than as a senior.

We emphasize the importance of career goals throughout this book. But that doesn't mean that all students settle on a career by the beginning of their second semester and, after that, it's smooth sailing. In fact, we believe choosing a career is a lifelong process. When you work summers in a law office, you get a first-hand feel for what the legal profession is like. This is much more valid experience than you'll get from watching reruns of *Perry Mason*. Developing a career means continually trying on roles to see how suitable they are to your interests and abilities. Do I like doing this? Can I do it well? And is there a future in it?

Part-time and summer work that is career related also helps you to refine your goals. Suppose you've known since high school that you wanted to work in a scientific/technical field. After some research you think that civil engineering might be for you. But which branch? Construction? Sewage disposal? Water treatment? Urban planning? Working in one or more of these areas can help you decide. And the sooner you get the experience, the sooner you'll know if it's right for you.

Career-related work enhances your academic experience. Sometimes it's difficult to see just how the theories in your textbooks can be put into practice. There can be a big gap between the ivory-tower atmosphere of school and the real-world problems encountered on the job. By working in your field of interest before you graduate, you can start to apply some of what you've learned in the classroom. And when you get back to school, many of your subjects become more relevant. You'll also have a better idea of what advanced electives to take.

Georgia Tech has had a co-op plan since 1912. Approximately twenty-two hundred students participate in the plan each year. Almost twice as many make the Dean's List as do students who aren't in co-op programs. Their work helps to make them better students.

One of the most valuable aspects of career-related work before you graduate is that you begin to develop the very skills and expertise that you will practice after you receive your degree. Do you want to make big bucks some day in sales? There's no better way to learn about selling than to start knocking on doors. Do you want to inspire a curiosity for learning in primary school children? Practice teaching will probably be your most useful experience. But don't wait until you're a senior to get a taste of it—find a job at a summer camp, a girls' club, or the YMCA. Do you want to be a plant manager? Try your hand on a production line for a while.

Many college students aspire to managerial positions someday. The sooner you get some supervisory experience, the better. A highly successful business consultant wryly related his son's first experience as a hotel management intern. The son had anticipated starting out behind the checkout counter. Instead, he was placed in charge of the cleanup crew in the main kitchen. He had to manage sixteen older, ethnically different, relatively uneducated men. It was a stressful internship for the student, but he learned an awful lot about people. He will have some very challenging questions to pose to his management profs when he returns to school. And he will be a much stronger job candidate when he eventually applies for a full-time job.

BE A STUDENT ENTREPRENEUR

We find that many college students want to own their own businesses someday. Well, you don't have to wait till you've saved up $50,000 seed money. You can start while you're still in school. In fact, there are students who establish flourishing enterprises even before they graduate.

Even if you don't plan on starting your own business in the future, starting a small one now can be an excellent way to develop new skills. The smallest undertaking can be a learning laboratory. In order to make a business go, you've got to come up with an idea and make that idea come to life. You've got to analyze the market, develop your products or services, market them, handle finances and accounting. If other people are involved, there are personnel questions to handle. And, of course, you've got to deal with your customers. Plus it's all *your* responsibility.

That sort of experience is music to an employer's ears. In many instances you can get academic credit for a business venture. And you can pick up some spare change, in some instances quite a lot of it. Mark McKee was the president of two companies by the end of his junior year at the University of Kansas. Pyramid Pizza earned $700,000 that year. Waddles Active Wear, which specializes in Hawaiian clothes, grossed $2 million. In 1986 Louis Kahn of Atlanta owned and operated a worldwide computer network, a computer mail-order catalog, a service for real-estate brokers, a small book publishing company, and an in-house ad agency. He was about to graduate from high school.

How do you get started? There is no one way. But students have made a go of all kinds of businesses—delivering munchies to dorm-rooms, bumper stickers, caps with messages, flower shops—we could go on for the next ten pages.

Larry Adler started by doing magic shows at kids' birthday parties. Then he started selling baskets full of favors at the same parties. Then he began distributing the baskets to retail stores. He phoned around to find better favors for his baskets. He was so impressed with one item that he asked if he could represent the company that manufactured it. He was told they already had a sales rep in the area where he lived. Could he be their sub-rep? Well, what would it hurt? Go ahead and try. His first month he won a set of matched luggage for being a sales leader. No one else in sales had ever been a leader for that company during their first month. Now he represents a number of companies that market children's products. He hopes to own a chain of Hallmark stores within three years. Larry says he's successful because he knows what kids will buy. He should—he's twelve years old.

For the mortals among you, consider first taking a course in entrepreneurship. Many universities offer them now. Join the Entrepreneur's Club on your campus. Read *The Student Entrepreneur's Guide*, by Brett Kingstone, and popular magazines such as *Enterprise*. Talk with other student entrepreneurs. Talk with your professors. But mainly, start thinking. Come up with a plan. And take action.

If you're convinced you need some money to get your business started, you can check into Venture Capital Network. For one hundred dollars and a completed application, your proposal will be entered into a computer and matched with investors with similar interests. It's a lot like computer dating. [Their address is P.O. Box 882, Durham, NH 03824. The phone number is (603) 862-3556.]

HOW TO GET A GOOD JOB WHILE YOU'RE STILL A STUDENT

It might seem like a tall order to find career-related employment when you're only eighteen or nineteen, but it can be done. Remember Larry Adler. Your school's co-operative plan or internship program is probably the path of least resistance, and we recommend both to you.

Co-op plans usually arrange ongoing, paid work alternating with school throughout the student's stay in college. By the time a student is in his last semester of work, he's usually making pretty good money. And he's earning it, because by now he has developed the skills that enable him to perform relatively sophisticated tasks.

Internships are more often one-time arrangements. Although many provide salaries, some offer only experience. If it's the right experience, it may still be invaluable. You know the old dilemma: you can't get a job without experience, but you can't get experience without a job. An internship may be your solution to the dilemma.

Internships also tend to draw less technically skilled students than do co-op plans. They provide an opportunity for someone to get a first exposure to a field, to try it on for size.

Even without the assistance of a formal program, you should be able to find some sort of job. In fact, landing a good job on your own is an impressive accomplishment and will be noted as such by future employers. Finding a job is a job in itself, and mastering the art of getting hired is a skill that most of you will use repeatedly throughout your lives. College graduates change jobs an average of eight times before they retire.

Read Chapters 12-16, which discuss the different phases of the job search. Pay special attention to "Resumes While Still In School" in Chapter 14 and "Questions Asked of Co-ops" in Chapter 15. The sort of job you can get depends a lot on how many skills you have already developed. But suppose you haven't developed many as yet. You're full of potential, but without much "actual."

Don't give up. It simply means that you're going to have to start at the bottom (better now than after graduation). Your first job may be as a gofer (go fer this, and then go fer that). But if you perform your menial duties enthusiastically and look for opportunities, you should be able gradually to assume some larger responsibilities. The idea is eventually to work yourself into a position that offers more challenge and fosters more professional growth.

In some cases you can earn academic credit along with your salary while you work. Sometimes you can get only one or the other. We recommend that you attempt to arrange some kind of credit. If there's no formal internship program on your campus, see what you can work out with your professors. We heard of one student who got academic credit while working as cashier in a convenience store. She observed that different types of people used the store at different hours of the day. She recorded her observations systematically and eventually turned them into a sociology report.

WHAT TO LOOK FOR IN A FIRST JOB

There are three things to consider—experience, experience, and experience. Naturally money is nice too. If you're working your way through college it's a necessity, but you usually won't be paid well without experience. Conversely, if you are paid well, it's probably because you're performing some important tasks for your employer. In other words, you're getting good experience.

Joan Macala, president of the Board of Directors of the National Society for Internships and Experiential Education, recommends that prospective interns first secure a written learning contract— what your duties will be, what skills you are to develop. Second, it's best if there are regular meetings with supervisors from both work and school. Finally, better internships include written evaluations of your performance and learning by you and your supervisor.

In conclusion, and at the risk of belaboring the point, get some career-related work experience. It is one of the very best ways you can invest in your own future.

SUMMARY

1. Employers value work experience, especially if it's career related.
2. Career-related experience teaches you about professional work.
3. Career-related experience helps you discover whether or not your chosen field suits you.
4. Career-related experience helps you to refine your professional goals.
5. Career-related work enhances your academic experience.
6. Career-related work enables you to develop the professional skills you will use after graduation.
7. Becoming a student entrepreneur is an excellent way to get experience.
8. Co-op plans and internships provide excellent opportunities for students to get their first career-related experience.

7
BPOC
(Big Person
On Campus)

Robert Blair, a senior business major with a 3.8 GPA, is slumped in his desk chair, staring at the wall. He's depressed. You would be too if you'd just received your fifth flush letter. He can't believe it, all those As, and still no plant trips. Meanwhile, Robert's roommate, Charles Neuberger, has already gotten two outright job offers. Charles has a few more Cs than Bs, and not very many As. How did he do it?

The answer is that Charles has developed people skills that you can't learn out of a book while Robert has avoided people by hiding behind books. Charles is a doer and a leader. He likes people, which is obvious every time he talks with a recruiter—his enthusiasm and self-assurance are catching.

Robert is shy, which is certainly no crime, but it definitely is a handicap. His parents and others tried to encourage him to break out of his shell, but he resisted their advice to get involved in campus life. He told himself that fraternities weren't for serious students. Student government never really did anything important. Professional societies on campus were just playing grown-up. And whenever he felt lonely, he could always read more or play with his computer.

During interviews he was ill at ease, and there were questions about his participation in campus activities that he couldn't answer. If he had wanted a position in pure research, the gaps in his experience might not have counted so heavily against him. Although even then he might have run into some problems—most employers want their technical people to have good communication skills. Besides, Robert wanted to be an executive. He wanted his first position to be his beginning step on the road to management.

One of the best ways to demonstrate that you're not one-dimensional is through your involvement in organizations. A recent survey conducted by AT&T indicated that participation in extracurricular activities was an excellent predictor of managerial potential. So, come job-hunting time, expect to be asked about what you did outside the classroom. If you did nothing, how will you explain this fact? Did you join several organizations, but only to pad your resume? A good interviewer will find out whether you were really involved or not. Did you hold an office? What were your duties? On which committees did you serve? What did you accomplish?

Rather than looking at campus involvement as more fodder for your resume, we recommend that you look at extracurricular activities as opportunities for personal development. Do you want to be an executive someday? Then lead a group or head up some project. Do you want to have a network of professional contacts? Then a good place to begin is through a student professional association. Through the right group you can also learn about different kinds of people and get exposure to new ideas.

We recommend that early on in your college career you identify one weakness or missing skill and try to develop it through some extracurricular activity.

And don't forget fun. You'll go nuts if you do nothing but chase success. What's the point of being successful if you never get any pleasure out of life? Besides, we are social animals. It is not likely that you will ever have a better opportunity for developing close, possibly lifelong friends than while you are in college. One of the best ways to meet people is through clubs and activities.

TYPES OF ACTIVITIES
Student Government

Through student government you can develop a number of skills that you'll use throughout your professional life: leadership, communication, persuasion, administration, negotiation. You learn through experience (there's that word again!) how things get done in an organization.

Do you want to establish a student course critique on your campus? It will take time and energy. You'll have to rally student, faculty, and administrative support in order to get the idea accepted. Compromises will have to be made. And once the legislation is passed, there's the not-so-small matter of implementation. Who develops the surveys? Who decides on the final format? How are they administered and scored? Who writes up the critique? How is it distributed? And how is the whole project funded?

By involving yourself in a project of this magnitude, you can learn things you just don't usually learn in a classroom. And, yes, it does look good on your resume and sound good during an interview.

The Greeks

Which statements are true? Fraternities are elitist, anti-intellectual gangs of juvenile delinquents masquerading as college students. Members live *in* animal houses, *on* alcohol, and *for* sex. Fraternities exist to promote the personal, social and intellectual development of their members. Sororities are clubs for superficial, air-headed snobs. Sororities promote sisterhood, service, and individual growth.

The answer, of course, is none of the above. And all of the above. There are no perfectly good or bad fraternities or sororities. Some are, however, better than others on any given campus. If you decide to join a Greek social organization, here are some things to look out for when you choose:

Does the group go in for hazing? If it does in any more than the mildest way, it's not likely going to help you succeed while you're in school or after you leave it. Studies have shown that the fraternities who go in for the heaviest hazing tend to have the lowest morale and to harbor the most hostility between members. Being a blue-chipper is competitive. You want to be a part of a group that reduces stress, not adds to it.

Does the group maintain a balance between social/recreational and academic activities? Of course, you want to have some fun, but you're also dead serious about success. Blue-chippers don't risk their future by joining an outfit that can't think past the next keg party. Some tip-offs to the ones that might work against you: The organization is perennially on academic or social probation. During rush, the actives never question you about grades or professional ambitions. None of the members are in demanding majors.

Another factor to consider is the kind of alumnus associated with the group. It can be a definite advantage to have a built-in connection to alumni who are leaders in business, government, science, and the arts. But not all Greek letter organizations have produced a list of VIP graduates. Find out if yours has before you sign on the dotted line and learn the secret handshake.

The advantages of being in a social organization are, first of all, friendship and fun. No one needs to apologize for wanting to have a good time with good friends. Moreover, if (and this is a big if) the brothers or sisters in your organization are also serious about career success, you can help each other reach your goals during college and throughout your life. A "good old boy" network can be a big professional asset until the day you retire. Increasingly, this is true of "good old girl" networks as well. But a network of bozos will not get you very far. A network of blue-chip brothers or sisters will.

Fraternities and sororities also expose you to the importance of teamwork. There has to be give and take for a Greek house to function effectively. By belonging to one, you learn when to pipe up and when to shut up, when to compromise and when to stick by your guns.

Most organizations offer the chance for you to lead. This is certainly true of the Greeks. Again, it's up to you to take advantage of this opportunity. Volunteer to head up the fund drive or to organize the spring picnic. And then do a good job. If you can do it right for the Phi Delta Sigmas, you may someday have the opportunity to do it right for IBM or for your own organization.

Professional Associations

We think most blue-chippers belong in a student professional association related to their intended career. Membership is probably not as valuable as career-related work, but it is a good supplement. The best source of knowledge about a career is from those who are successfully practicing it. Professional societies expose you to just such people.

You will also meet other students who share your goals. Pre-meds, pre-laws, and student entrepreneurs can support and encourage each other. It's a good place to form friendships since you have at least one thing in common.

If you take advantage of it, there should also be the opportunity to gain leadership experience. And it never hurts to list an office that you held on your resume.

One of the main advantages to joining a professional association is to extend your network of contacts (see Chapter 8). We know of one student who made it a point to see to the arrangements for everyone who spoke to his group. In some instances he picked them up at the airport and shuttled them back. This might seem like a nuisance, but it afforded him the chance to spend a lot of time alone with leaders in his field.

He could ask any question he wanted about his intended profession and get it answered in detail by an expert. He could try out new ideas and get them critiqued. Soon he began exchanging business cards and corresponding with these same people. By the time he graduated he had developed professional relationships with some very impressive folks.

Community Service

The Peace Corps recruits its volunteers differently than it used to. It now emphasizes the skills that can be developed on a tour, skills that will be highly marketable to employers when the volunteer's service is completed. Of course, working for the Peace Corps or Vista has always afforded opportunities for professional development. And so does working as a Candy Striper, tutoring underprivileged children, visiting geriatric residents, and organizing recreational activities for patients in a mental hospital.

Community service is another way to get experience. And experience is still the best way to learn about a field, develop professionally related skills, and fatten your resume. It also affords you a different kind of experience—the chance to learn about people who are very different from you.

College is supposed to teach you about the world; yet it can be very provincial in its own ivory-tower way. In most college settings you are denied contact with the very old, the poor, the sick, the unsuccessful.

You are similarly shielded from these segments of the population in the business community. Community service, then, exposes you to more of the world and gives you the opportunity to help make it a better one.

Groups Based on Age, Sex, or Race

From 1636, when Harvard University was founded, until the end of World War II in 1945, the vast majority of American college students were single white males between the ages of eighteen and twenty-two. Most came from well-to-do families. American higher education still has a ways to go before it serves all segments of our population equally, but students today are definitely a more varied lot.

There are now slightly more women than men on college campuses. More students are over the age of twenty-five, and a fair number are over forty. There are more blacks, Hispanics, and native Americans. There are also immigrants from all over the world, as well as a significant number of foreign students.

In the midst of all this diversity, it is very easy for any one student to feel lost and out of place. Assuming that your hearing is good, imagine for a moment what it would be like to attend a college for the hearing impaired. Lectures would be signed instead of spoken. Not knowing sign language, you would feel lost in class and be a stranger in the residence halls.

While most of you won't face barriers that are this extreme, you may well face problems in adjusting that can interfere with your ability to learn. Even well-intentioned people tend to notice differences before similarities. You may be recognized more for the color of your skin, the sound of your accent, or the gray in your hair than for your intelligence and drive. As paradoxical as it sounds, probably the majority of you are one kind of minority or another.

Your chances for success in college improve when you're convinced you belong there. But it's hard to feel as if you fit in when you're a black student in a sea of white faces. Or a mother of children older than most of your classmates. How do you develop a social life? Who do you date if you're single? Who will understand your customs without your first having to explain them? Because of these factors some students feel more comfortable attending a college with a student body more like themselves. Some blacks seem to develop more rapidly on historically black campuses. Apparently, they are even better equipped to adjust to a predominantly white professional setting after graduation. Some women seem to prosper similarly by attending a women's college.

The majority of you will attend coeducational colleges that are racially mixed. Most of these schools have organizations in which membership is based upon ethnic background (Afro-American Association), a common experience (a veterans' organization), gender (Society of Women Engineers), or age (a group for mid-life career changers). We believe it is important for you eventually to be comfortable with a variety of individuals and settings. But joining a group of students who share your cultural heritage may be an important first step in feeling at home on your campus. Groups whose focus is religious (Baptist Student Union), political (Young Democrats), or issue-oriented (Green Peace) can also serve this function. Moreover, participation in such groups enables you to express yourself in ways unrelated to your career, and that's important too.

Student Athletics

We're talking about the *business* of intercollegiate athletics here, not intramural flag football between the dorms and the frats. If you're in a revenue-producing sport at a Division I school, you've probably convinced yourself that you're going to be one of the elite group who makes it in the pros. You're probably very wrong. (Our apologies if you're the next Michael Jordan or John Elway.) Most student athletes never make a nickel in professional sports. Most of those who do last only a few years and don't make megabucks. Those are the hard, cold facts.

There are some advantages to playing intercollegiate sports, but first, let us tell you about the obstacles they pose to your becoming a blue-chip graduate. The typical day of a student athlete begins at 6 A.M. with a strategy session, followed by mandatory breakfast at 7. There will probably be classes during most of the morning since the afternoon will be taken up with the sport. Weight training and organized practice can take five or six exhausting hours a day. Not much time or energy is left for studies, and there is virtually none for other extracurricular activities. It is against NCAA regulations for a scholarship athlete to work for pay while enrolled in school, so career-related work experience is very difficult to come by. Most summers, athletes are enrolled in school and busy with weight training.

So, how does a student athlete refine his career choice? Develop marketable skills? Make professional contacts? Get a taste of working in his field? Keep her grades up? (Increasingly, there are scholarships available for women athletes.) The answer is that it's very difficult. You really have to be on your toes if you want to be a blue-chip graduate.

Here are some suggestions about how you can maximize your chances if you're a student athlete:

Time management is crucial. Get organized quickly, and stay organized. Take complete advantage of tutorial and advisory assistance provided for student athletes. But don't stop there. Get to know your professors. Find out from them how you can improve your performance. Attend your classes. Sit front and center. Participate. Try to develop marketable skills through your athletics. Be enthusiastic. Show up on time. Demonstrate good work habits during practice. Show that you're a leader.

Get to know influential alumni and athletic supporters. No, we're not talking about money under the table. This is one of the best ways for you to make professional contacts. Let the alumnus or booster know that you're interested in his business, that you want to be successful off the field as well as on it. You won't be able to co-op, but you should be able to work out some kind of internship in your field for academic credit that will also give you some all-important experience. A series of part-time internships over the summers may be a possibility. You can keep your grades up, get exposure to your career, and keep the NCAA happy. Another option is to do a full-time internship after your athletic eligibility is over, but before you graduate. (It is not likely that a student athlete will graduate in just four years.)

And now for the advantages of playing a varsity sport. First, you'll be doing something you enjoy a great deal. In fact, don't even consider playing a college sport unless you love it. The sacrifices are too great. The pay is terrible. Sure, you get tuition, room, and board, but you have to give up as many as sixty hours a week to your sport. It is probably much easier to work your way through school waiting tables or selling shoes than to do so on an athletic scholarship. Second, if you're in the right program, sports can build character, teach teamwork, develop leadership. We live in a competitive society. You can learn to compete. Third, there are opportunities for contacts if you take advantage of them.

Intercollegiate athletics, then, can be a plus. But if you're not careful, they can be a one-way street to a tainted degree or no degree at all. Two questions to ask of any athletic program: How many student athletes graduate? And how many student athletes are involved in successful careers after their playing days are over?

Groups For The Fun Of It

Yes, college is serious business, but it should also be a blast. We think it's a good idea to get involved in some activities not because you'll make contacts, not because you're developing some highly marketable skill, but simply because they're fun and you'll make some friends. Having a good time at least some of the time is not a luxury; it's a necessity for your physical and mental health. There are hundreds of groups which center around hobbies and recreational pursuits. They range from racketball to rock climbing, from wine tasting to woodworking, from sailing to singing, from band to backgammon. So take your pick. Just for the fun of it.

SUMMARY

1. Don't limit your education to the classroom.
2. Use campus activities to your advantage.
3. Develop people skills and other marketable abilities that employers look for.
4. Make contacts and close friends.
5. Learn about your career.
6. Enjoy yourself and have a good time.

8
It's Who You Know: Building Contacts

What student wouldn't love to get a glowing recommendation from a professor for a job or graduate fellowship? Or have some highly placed manager or entrepreneur make an unsolicited job offer. And wouldn't it be nice to have an expert in your field show you the ropes and help you on your way to a successful career?

OK, so you want important people on your side. Fine, but do you realize that it's up to you to make this happen? This chapter tells you how.

We advise students to start building their network of contacts the first day of their freshman year, or better yet, while they're still in high school. We often get resistance on this point along several lines:

Why would important people want to bother with me? Because it comes with the territory. Experts and people in power expect requests for information and assistance. Because most successful people want to help you succeed. This is especially true if they're convinced you're seriously committed to success. Because you make it worth their while. Life is give and take. If you help others, they'll usually help you. And if you're wondering what on earth you can do to help an older, established professional, we'll tell you later on in this chapter.

Isn't it insincere or maybe even downright manipulative to cultivate relationships for the sole purpose of advancing your career? Not at all. Most business relationships are just that—relationships that exist for the mutual benefit of both parties. Naturally, it's nicer if friendship develops as well, but it's not necessary. One word of warning, however; don't settle for having only a network of contacts. You need friends as well—people who accept you for who you are and not just what you can do for them.

Won't it detract from my success if I get help from others? Don't kid yourself. You can use a helping hand. We all can. This doesn't mean you get people to do for you what you can just as easily do for yourself. But, as you'll see in Chapter 12, achievers take advantage of every resource in their environment. They actively seek out other people who can help them reach their goals. Don't waste ten years reinventing the wheel when you can buy tires at any service station in town.

But what if I'm shy? I have a hard enough time asking my roommate if I can borrow two sheets of typing paper. How am I going to ask some big shot to take time out of his busy schedule for me? Shyness can be a big obstacle to your success, so we urge you to take steps to overcome it. Use your campus resources (see Chapter 10): attend an assertiveness training workshop, take a speech class, get some counseling. In general, you can develop self-confidence by taking a series of small, gradually more difficult steps: next time ask your roommate for three sheets of paper.

Blue-chippers develop a network of contacts:
1. Experts who can provide information or assistance;
2. People in the know who can give you job leads;
3. Persons in power who can open doors;
4. Mentors who can do a little of all three plus provide general support as well.

Information and Assistance

One of the best ways to learn about a field or a particular profession is to talk with experts who are leaders in that area. We told you how to go about doing that in Chapter 5. We think it's a good idea to keep track of these folks by entering them in your address book. As your list grows over the years, you'll find that your wallet-sized book won't accommodate everybody. Or you won't be able to remember exactly what type of information this particular person can provide. At some point you'll want to organize your list of contacts better.

So you get a larger address book or index-card file box which you keep in your office. (Students can have offices too, even if they consist only of a well-organized desk in a dormitory room.) Now, in addition to addresses and phone numbers, you'll start to keep a little information about this person—the dates when you talked and what you talked about, the person's position or title, and what organization the person is affiliated with.

Experts can be business leaders or professors. They may be other students. They can be friends of your family or members of your church or temple. You may need information about a prospective career, about a topic for a term paper, or the best place to stay at Ft. Lauderdale over spring break. The important thing is they have the information you need.

Helpful people can also provide assistance: how to solve a physics problem, a loan to tide you over for the last couple weeks of a school term, the key resource book you need to write your term paper. They can be a part of your overall support system.

Job Leads

As you will see in Chapter 14, contacts can tell you where the jobs are. In fact, many career experts believe this is the best way to find a good job. Of course, it is important that you build your network of contacts all along the way so that you can call on them when it's time to look for a job.

Opening Doors

Experts are frequently in positions of power, and it is a huge plus to have powerful people on your side. If it's nice to get a lead on a good job, it's even nicer when someone with clout will recommend you highly for that job. And it's nicer still when such a person actually hires you. Similarly, it's a great help when someone can pave the way for a loan to start up your small business. And it's best of all when that person himself will agree to be your financial backer.

Mentors

If you put all of these roles together and add some personal interest in your success, you've got a mentor. Highly successful people often point to a key teacher or leader who advised, guided, supported, and pushed them on their way. Plato had Socrates. Aristotle had Plato. Bill Curry, head football coach at Alabama, was coached over the course of his playing career by Bobby Dodd, Vince Lombardi, and Don Shula. If you're not a sports fan, that's analogous to a novice musician being personally taught by Bach, Mozart, and Beethoven.

One of the best ways to learn something is by watching an expert do it right. Psychologists call this vicarious learning, and it's something you don't want to miss out on. Just think what it would be like for a budding engineer to apprentice to a Leonardo da Vinci, a novice manager to work for a Lee Iacocca, a beginning nurse to follow a Florence Nightingale on her rounds. Obviously, not everyone can study at the feet of a master, but just about everyone can find teachers and leaders who are farther along the road to success than they are themselves. It could be a professor or dean. It could be an employer. It might be the senior down the hall who's the top pre-med on campus or who's already a successful student entrepreneur.

But how do you get these people to help out little old you? We're glad you asked that. Listen up, because we're going to tell you.

Steps in Forming A Mentor Relationship

1. *Show them you're committed to success.* Before people take you on as a protege, they want to know that you're a winner. You've got to convince them you've got the talent and drive to make spending time with you worth their while.

Representatives from student organizations often make requests of professors, civic leaders, and people in business. Will you teach our fraternity pledge class study skills? Can you give a talk on investment banking to our professional association? Could you conduct a resume workshop for our organization?

Even if they're not particularly critical, we have observed that professionals automatically form impressions of every student who makes the request and handles the arrangements. Does the student ask far enough ahead of time for the expert to clear his schedule? If not, the professional will assume the student doesn't know how to manage his time. He will also resent the implication that he, the professional, has so little to do that, of course, he can adjust his schedule at the last minute for the convenience of the student.

Has the student thought through her request carefully enough so that she can state it clearly? Notice the difference between: A.) Our group has a lot of liberal arts majors. Last year's seniors didn't do very well at finding good jobs. Could you talk to us about how we could improve our chances? and B.) We need someone to talk to us about getting good jobs.

An expert will have a much better chance of delivering a timely, relevant message to group A than to group B. She will also be inclined to regard the representative of group A as brighter, more conscientious, and more mature.

Do the students follow through? Do they meet the speaker when she gets there? Do they have the overhead slide projector ready to go? Did they take the trouble to drum up a crowd? Do they send a letter of thanks? Is it well written?

Since so many students fail to observe minimal standards of professional courtesy, you have to behave truly abysmally to distinguish yourself as a real loser. For the same reason, it is easy to show yourself to be a winner. By simply being considerate of the professionals you deal with, you stand out as a blue-chipper.

Every college class you take provides you with an opportunity to demonstrate to a professor that you've got the "right stuff." Turning in quality work is an obvious first step, but don't stop there. Attend class and be punctual. Perhaps most important is that you participate in class. No, don't speak up just to hear yourself talk, but do contribute to the class discussion. If you don't understand something, ask for an explanation. An intelligent question usually gets a good answer. It also shows that you were intelligent for asking the question. Come prepared. If you've read yesterday's class notes and today's chapter, you're more prepared than most students. But your professors won't know this unless you speak up.

Many of you are attending large state universities and community colleges. Classes often have several hundred students in them. Graduating seniors sometimes can't identify a single professor who knows them well enough to write a decent recommendation. Don't get caught in that predicament. If you go to a big school, make it a point for at least one professor in your field to know you well and to think well of you.

You accomplish this by making an *A* and writing the best term paper or final exam the prof ever saw. At least that's what you try for. This should also be the class that you never miss and you're always prepared for. And no matter how shy you are, force yourself to participate in class discussions. You may not be someone with a 1300 SAT score and a 3.7 GPA. If you're working your way through school, you may not have much time for your studies. But surely you can concentrate doubly hard on at least one class.

The same principles apply on the job. Remember Chapter 6. Whether you're co-oping, interning, or working part-time—show someone in power that you're a blue-chipper. Not, not by apple-polishing, brown-nosing, or toadying. As the saying goes, "You do it the old-fashioned way. You earn it." You earn it by showing up on time every day, working hard, and volunteering for extra work.

2. *Make it worth their while.* When you search for a mentor, you're looking for someone who will teach you, guide you, and help you. It's nice if someone volunteers for the job, but most people you'd want to learn from are busy, busy, busy. Usually they'll help you if you help them. Generally it's up to you to take the first step.

Volunteer to assist your prospective mentor with his work. Many professors do research and could use someone to tally scores or collate data. Out on the job, managers, project engineers, head nurses, etc., can generally use a helping hand. And so can presidents of sororities, professional societies, and student governments.

When you do volunteer to help, do your best. Do a bang-up job. Go the second mile. Demonstrate some loyalty.

3. *Expect the relationship to evolve gradually.* It usually takes a while for a mentor to warm up to you enough to take you under her wing. And after a solid relationship is established, it should continue to evolve. As you learn more and more from your mentor, you should gradually be accorded greater responsibility. The idea is to work toward becoming a colleague, not a lackey.

It sometimes happens that your prospective mentor doesn't want to take you on. No matter how hard you try, he brushes you off. Try not to take it personally. Maybe he's too busy, he's already mentoring too many other aspiring blue-chippers, or he's just not a very helpful person.

At some point your persistence becomes bullheadedness, and you're better off trying with someone else. As we said earlier, not everyone can have Lee Iacocca. Nor is the biggest shot around necessarily your best prospect. Sometimes a less visible person has more time to give and a better disposition for doing so.

As you become more successful yourself, don't forget all the help you got along the way. We think one of the best ways to show your gratitude is by helping those who are just starting their own journey.

SUMMARY

1. It's to your advantage to have a network of contacts.
2. It's up to you to build the network.
3. Start your freshman year.
4. Establish relationships with successful people by showing them you're committed to success and by helping them.
5. Cultivate relationships with professors, professionals in your field, and other students.
6. You can find helpful people in many places, including: classes, professional organizations, campus activities, and at work.
7. Develop a filing system for keeping track of your contacts.
8. If possible, find a mentor who will help guide you on your road to success.

9
Keeping Calm
Under Pressure &
Making Sense Of It All

If you've read this far, you're probably serious about becoming a blue-chip graduate. You want as good a job as you can get, and this book tells you how to do it. Just remember, career fulfillment is made up of many things. Money and prestige are only two of them. Don't make the mistake of majoring in Pre-Wealth! At least not to the exclusion of everything else.

Howard Hughes's billions didn't prevent him from being miserable. Phil Donahue's examination of life in a wealthy Texas suburb on network TV revealed a depressing emptiness behind the facade of expensive cars and designer clothes.

Occasionally, students ask us which branch of engineering offers the highest salaries. A few of these students want to choose their life's work on the basis of dollars alone. Actually, this doesn't even make good financial sense. The demand for graduates in different fields changes from year to year. Right now electrical engineering and investment banking are hot. They may not be ten years from now. How ironic it would be to commit to a field you hate and have it dry up on you before you turn thirty.

Besides, extrinsic rewards less often foster creative results than intrinsic ones. Research by Brandeis University's Teresa Amabile indicates that being interested in your work may be the single most important factor in a creative outcome. And it is the creative results that bring in the top dollar. So learn to live with the following paradox: working only for money often stifles creativity; yet creativity is usually rewarded monetarily. We think it's smart to consider the financial prospects a field offers, but not to the exclusion of everything else. Find work that you like. It will pay off in many ways.

Focusing solely on the steps of your career ladder tends to produce tunnel vision. In today's rapidly changing world you need a broader view in order to be successful in your profession and in life. You need the liberal arts, social sciences, and fine arts as well as business and technical knowledge. You need more than smarts—you need wisdom.

If it is unwise to equate success with income, it is equally unwise to make your self-worth equal to your success. To do so breeds fear of failure, and that undermines your willingness to take risks. If you can't respect yourself after a failure, you can expect anxiety, depression, and stress as your constant companions. Some students panic when they first see the Four-Year Master Plan (Appendix I). How can they possibly get everything done? They feel overwhelmed.

Remember, there is no "must" in the Master Plan. You don't have to do any of it. If you manage to pull off half of it, you're probably well ahead of most other college students. The Master Plan is not an end in itself; it's only a set of guidelines. And when all is said and done they boil down to a few practical suggestions: Get organized. Whether you study five hours a week or twenty-five, use the most effective techniques. Clarify your goals. Get some work experience. Make some contacts. Use your campus resources. Learn how to find a job.

You can be competitive without becoming hooked on competition for its own sake. Some of you may prefer being a bigger fish in a smaller pond. Is an Ivy League degree really worth it if you have to wreck your family's finances to get it? Not everyone is necessarily happier at IBM than at Joe's Electronics. There are blue-chip graduates who go into law, medicine, and investment banking. Others join the Peace Corps, teach public school, or enter social work. Still others practice their craft in an artist's studio or on a stage.

STRESS MANAGEMENT CHECKLIST

1. Manage your time and organize your things—two sure ways to reduce your headaches and save your stomach lining.

2. Don't spread yourself too thin. See number 3.

3. Learn to say "no." See number 2.

4. Cultivate friends as well as contacts.

5. Participate in at least one extracurricular activity because you enjoy it, not because it's going to pay off down the road.

6. Do something fun every day.

7. Exercise regularly. The busier you are, the more important this one is.

8. Eat sensibly.

9. Get enough sleep.

10. Learn to relax. We've included instructions at the end of this chapter for Deep Muscle Relaxation and Guided Imagery, but biofeedback, yoga, and meditation are also effective tension reducers for most people.

Read this checklist every day for a week. Read it every week for a month. Read it every month for a year. Repeat as needed.

Recently we heard a psychologist refer to the very competitive university where he worked as a Type-A factory. Type-A individuals are goal directed, driven people who get a lot done, but find it difficult to relax. They are also heart attack prone.

Recent research by health psychologist Margaret Chesney, however, suggests that it is possible to be achievement oriented without the heart attack. The key is in your attitude. Anger and hostility seem to be much more injurious to your heart than ambition and hard work. The most deadly combination of all is the Type A who is unassertive and very angry. He's too passive to get his own way very often, so he spends a lot of time feeling frustrated and mad. And because he lacks the ability to express himself assertively, he has no constructive way of communicating his pent-up feelings.

It would appear, then, that you can strive toward your goals if you're flexible about doing so. Frequent frustration and anger are the tip-offs that you're not keeping things in perspective. *If blue-chip college life seems too hectic, see a counselor.*

In conclusion, we offer two final bits of advice. Repeat them whenever the stress starts to mount:

DON'T SWEAT THE SMALL STUFF.

IT'S ALL SMALL STUFF!

Deep Muscle Relaxation Instructions

Find a quiet place and get into a comfortable position. Your bed or an easy chair is usually conducive to relaxing. Take your time when you practice DMR. Hurrying defeats the purpose. After you get more skilled at relaxing you can learn to speed the technique up. Most people get better results if they close their eyes while practicing this technique.

1. Make tight fists out of both your hands. Study the tension in your hands. Now, let it go. Allow every muscle fibre in your hands to grow limp and calm. Notice that we say "allow." You can't really relax by trying harder.

2. Repeat this pattern with each muscle group in your body. Next, do your forearms.
3. Upper arms.
4. Shoulders and neck.
5. Forehead.
6. Eyes.
7. Lips.
8. Jaw.
9. Chest.
10. Abdomen.
11. Upper legs.
12. Lower legs.
13. Feet.

The entire exercise should take ten or more minutes, but with practice you can learn to relax in seconds.

Guided Imagery Instructions

Find a quiet, comfortable place and close your eyes. Imagine that you're resting securely on a beautiful, deserted beach. Beyond the white sand is azure water with gentle, rolling waves. Feel the warmth of the sun on your skin, the caress of the breeze in your hair, the grainy texture of the sand between your toes. Relax. Listen to the sound of the surf. Watch the rhythm of the waves as they rise and fall. Take in a deep breath of fresh salt air and relax deeply as you exhale. Notice a flock of gulls hovering above the waves. Study the slow, graceful movement of the wings of one of the birds. Watch the bird's wings gradually slow down. Yet it stays airborne, seemingly without effort. Become as relaxed as the bird.

Again the entire fantasy should take ten or more minutes. Following DMR with a relaxing mental scene often deepens the sense of calm, so experiment with combining the two methods. Practice is, of course, essential. Remember, relaxation isn't a luxury. It's a necessity. Money and position mean very little if you're not healthy.

Using Relaxation Techniques Situationally

Relax by using DMR or imagery. Once you're calm and tension-free, you can prepare for any stressful task, such as a test or important interview. Simply imagine yourself handling the test effectively. Should you start to feel any tension or anxiety, redirect your attention to the beach scene (or whatever scene is most relaxing to you) until you regain your composure. Keep repeating until you can easily imagine yourself handling the task in question.

On the day of the test, be sure to show up at class on time. While the test is being passed out, quietly relax using the techniques you've mastered. Should you get flustered or find your mind racing during the test, simply pause and take a couple of minutes to relax.

SUMMARY

1. Plan a career that interests and challenges you. Money is an important consideration, but not the only one.
2. Don't equate external success with internal fulfillment.
3. Make the principles embodied in the Stress Management Checklist an integral part of your life.
4. The Master Plan is a set of guidelines, not the Ten Commandments.
5. It is not ambition that causes heart attacks, but unbridled ambition.
6. Learn Deep Muscle Relaxation and/or Guided Imagery.
7. Learn how to apply these relaxation techniques situationally.
8. If you feel you are under too much stress, get some help. See a counselor.

10
Your Secret Goldmine: Campus Resources

Imagine that scattered around your campus are several large boxes stuffed with cash. Whenever your funds run low, you're free to drop by one of these handy mini-banks and help yourself. That's right, all you have to do is scoop up enough fives and tens to keep you in cheeseburgers and books for another month.

You'd expect these financial "free lunch" dispensers to get a lot of use, wouldn't you? Who could possibly be so dense as to miss out on such an opportunity? Yet agencies doling out thousands of dollars worth of services are often passed over by the majority of college students.

Ah, but that's different, you say. Money is money. Deans and counselors are somehow less appealing. Maybe so, but reflect for a moment on what money really is. You can't eat it or wear it. It doesn't even burn well enough to keep you warm. But you can trade it for food, clothing, and fuel. And also for books and tuition. Or for legal or medical advice. Or tutoring or psychotherapy. Or any of a dozen other services designed to help you become a blue-chip graduate. And once you're a blue-chip graduate, any number of employers will pay you lots of money so that you can choose to buy whichever goods and services your heart desires.

Blue-chippers, in their drive for excellence, don't pass up free help. They do take advantage of every opportunity and resource in their environment which will advance them toward their goals. We'll tell you more about what makes achievers tick in the next chapter. For now, trust us that this chapter is worth your while.

Most students are surprised when they learn about all the services that are available to them. We recommend that at your earliest convenience you carefully review your student handbook or the appropriate section of your college catalog. Then start using your campus resources. And if your school doesn't offer a service that you need, see if you can find it elsewhere. Remember, it's up to you to get whatever help you require to succeed. Nobody is going to rescue you.

PRIMARY RESOURCES
Library Services

The computer is transforming the way the modern library does its business. On-line databases have revolutionized traditional research techniques. Instead of wading through endless card files, going blind in front of the microfiche, and struggling through reference books the size of cinder blocks, you can do an instant information search by punching in a few key words. Libraries can lease or purchase a database on just about any subject, including popular magazines, business and trade periodicals, scholarly abstracts, financial resources, conference proceedings, and high-tech journals. Some libraries, such as the one at Northeast Missouri State University, link with others through an on-line cataloging system and provide access to almost unlimited information.

The compact disc is another high-tech innovation that expedites data retrieval. DATEXT and CORPTECH are two compact disc systems that provide information on companies and their executives. Many libraries offer instructional modules on videotape. And some provide assistance in writing term papers and offer seminars on research techniques. Increasingly, there are services and facilities for students with physical disabilities or language barriers.

Check with your library to see exactly what is available. Get to know a librarian or two. As a budding blue-chipper, you'll want to take advantage of all of this assistance.

The College Catalog

Here is another storehouse of useful information. Granted, it's not exactly a page-turner, but you can save a lot of time and trouble if you use this resource regularly. Almost every day students ask us questions that they could easily answer themselves by checking their catalogs. Sioux is particularly keen on double-checking rules and regulations. She should be. She had to leave town just before her graduation. Several months later she learned that she had not been granted a degree because she was short three courses. (There had been a miscommunication about her requirements.) But it was Sioux that had to pay the extra tuition to make up the work. Your school probably provides additional handbooks on student life and services as well. You should also take advantage of the information they contain.

Financial Aid

As long as the cost of a college education continues to rise, so will the need for financial aid. For example, during the fall of 1984, 98 percent of full-time freshmen at Penn State university were assisted.

There are three main types of aid—scholarships (or grants), loans, and student employment. They come from four different sources—colleges, the private sector, federal, and state governments. In general, most awards are based on need, but a fair number are based on merit (athletic, academic, talent, etc.). Federal aid to education is currently a hotly contested political issue. We anticipate that there will continue to be some sort of governmental financial aid, but it is difficult to say whether programs will increase or decrease.

Apply early. Fall of your senior year in high school is best, but it's never too late. If you miss out one year, you can try for the following one. Talk with your financial aid office to find out what is offered by your school and how to apply for it. They maintain information on all federal and state programs and often have impressive files on funding from the private sector. By belonging to a particular religious, minority, special interest, or ethnic group, you may qualify for scholarships. But you'll never know what the criteria are unless you check them out.

The Counseling Center

College life is hardly ever the four-year beer bust that the media portray. You might as well face the fact that college can be stressful. You could have a professor capable of sedating an insomniac. Your roommate might turn out to be the missing link. You're busier than you've ever been with less guidance than you've ever had. You're trying to break away from your parents, but you're still homesick. You have to make big-league decisions about majors and careers, and you're competing against some pretty sharp cookies. Small wonder that, after drunk driving, suicide is the number-one killer of college students. Eating disorders are rampant among coeds. And many students needlessly suffer depression and anxiety, loneliness and guilt. We say needlessly because most colleges provide free psychological services for their students.

There still seems to be a stigma attached to getting counseling, but our impression is that there are two kinds of students—those who can admit they need help and those who can't. This is not to say there are loads of emotional basket cases running around. Most students manage to get by. It's just that there's probably some kind of psychological service that can make life a lot easier for the vast majority of you. And the price is right because it's generally free. Once you graduate, therapy can easily run into thousands of dollars.

There is usually help for academic, vocational, personal, and social problems. Services include individual and group counseling, testing, and career information. Many universities provide couples' counseling whether you're married, living together, or just dating. Increasingly, computer-assisted instruction is available. (Two examples are SIGI for vocational decision making, put out by Educational Testing Service, and CASSI-GT, a study skills package put out by Georgia Tech.)

A staple of most counseling centers is outreach and psycho-education. Typical workshops and seminars include assertiveness, life-planning, dating skills, overcoming shyness, autohypnosis, time-management, dream interpretation, test anxiety reduction, study skills, career exploration, and self-esteem elevation. Some of these offerings provide great ways to develop marketable skills. Some make your life go a lot smoother. Others are simply stimulating and fun. If you haven't used the counseling center in some way before you graduate, you're probably cheating yourself.

New Student Orientation

College is different than high school. It is usually harder, bigger, and faster. You may be on your own for the first time. Or years may have passed since you last were a student, and you have less academic self-confidence than your professor has mercy. Aside from a few rules to keep dormitories marginally civilized, you can pretty much do what you want—including sleeping in, cutting classes, and never cracking a book—and no one will seem to care. If you flunk out, there will be another warm body to replace you. Isn't it obvious that you're better off knowing what to expect and how to cope with it?

In addition to handling college life, there is the matter of handling the particular college that you attend. Where are the buildings, the agencies, the administrators on your campus? And exactly what services are offered? What is expected of you?

Well, you can breathe a little easier because virtually all schools provide some kind of orientation for freshmen and transfer students. Most are voluntary programs, and we urge you to attend. Bluechippers don't pass up free help.

Orientation programs range in length from one day in the summer to several days immediately preceding the beginning of the term to a semester-long course for credit. Whether you consider yourself a strong student or a weak one, we recommend that you take the course if it's available. You'll get an in-depth treatment of how to succeed academically and usually some solid information about adjusting to the rigors of college life. The briefer orientation programs cover the school's academic structure and regulations, class schedules, campus services and facilities, resident hall life, commuter student issues, and social activities. You'll hear from assorted faculty and staff. You might get to sit in on a live or simulated class. Many schools provide parallel sessions for parents to address their particular concerns.

If your school doesn't offer an orientation program, contact the office of student services for more information.

Legal Services

Your landlord says that you owe $150 in back rent, and you say you don't. You don't want to part with the $150, but you don't have Perry Mason to argue your case. What are you going to do?

Most schools will offer some kind of legal assistance to their students. Generally, legal counselors are available to answer questions and handle simple legal matters—such as disputes over lease agreements. If you find yourself in more serious trouble, the counselors can refer you to an attorney in the community. If your college doesn't provide this service, discuss your concerns with the Dean of Students. You might also consider your community's legal aid service.

Military Organizations

The armed services offer some very generous scholarships. The military is also an avenue for developing leadership and other marketable skills. You are, of course, obligated to a certain number of years of service, so it is not a commitment to make lightly. Your choice of major has a strong bearing on which branch of the military will accept you. Engineers have a better chance with the Air Force. Liberal arts majors have the best chance with the Navy and Marine Corps, less with the Army, and least with the Air Force. For more information about ROTC programs, service academies, and tuition credit take a look at *How The Military Will Help You Pay for College*, by Don M. Berrerton (Peterson's Guides: Princeton, NJ, 1985).

Resources For Entrepreneurs

As student interest in entrepreneurial activities has risen, so has official support by American universities. Most schools with business colleges offer coursework related to small business management or entrepreneurism. A few schools, such as Babson College, The University of Southern California, and Baylor University offer degree programs. If there's nothing official going on where you're enrolled, talk with some of the business faculty. Get them to arrange an internship or course credit for a business venture you want to start. At the very least, get all the free consultation you can from your professors.

Several organizations for entrepreneurs are affiliated with universities. They regularly hold conferences, produce newsletters, or sponsor seminars. Contact any of the following for more information:

Caruth Institute for Owner-Managed Business
Southern Methodist University
Dallas, TX 75265-9990
214/692-3326;

International Council for Small Business (ICSB)
U.S. Affiliate Office: ICSB-US
Brooks Hall
University of Georgia
Athens, GA 30602
(Written requests only);

Journal of Small Business Management
Bureau of Business Research
West Virginia University
P.O. Box 6025
Morgantown, WV 26505-6025
304/2443-5837.

The Placement Center

Placement can be one of your strongest allies in getting a job. Their main function on campus is to serve as an employment agency. If your school is large, prestigious, or has many marketable majors, chances are that the placement center will be inundated with recruiters—which means more opportunities for you. Most placement centers are more than a clearing house for employers to meet candidates. They will also offer workshops or consultation on resume construction and interviewing skills. On some campuses placement will help you plan your career from day one—which means you should call on them your freshman year.

Developmental/Remedial Studies

Some students get to State U. only to discover that they're not ready for college work. The reason is not important for our purposes. The solution is. If you believe you're in over your head, it is very easy to get down on yourself and feel ashamed and stupid. Or you can blame public education, your parents, or your high-school math teacher for your miserable state. Neither course of action will get you very far because neither course really involves any action.

Most campuses have some agency to help you if you're academically underdeveloped or disadvantaged. *Don't be too proud to use their services.* Here you'll find study skills programs, tutoring, preparatory classes, and lots of moral support. You might be a whiz in science and math, but a wimp in reading and writing. There's no law that says you can't take differential equations and remedial composition at the same time.

Campus Ministries

There is currently a revival of interest in religious issues among college students. If you want to be active in a church or temple, you'll probably find an organization to meet your needs. In many cases there are full-time clergy staffing an impressive facility and a variety of programs. In others there are volunteers who arrange meetings in dorm rooms. As the saying goes, "Seek and you shall find."

Health Clinic

Most colleges have one. Sooner or later, almost every college student needs one. They range from a single nurse in an office on some small campuses to a full-scale medical center with in-patient facilities at some large universities. Many will continue to administer a medical regimen for you that your private physician has prescribed. Some offer psychiatric care. Some have programs dealing with eating disorders, reproduction and contraception, sexually transmitted diseases, and substance abuse among others. Read your catalog or student handbook to find out exactly what's available at the clinic on your campus.

Recreation and Physical Fitness

Most colleges have buildings and equipment that would make your high-school gym class look like a dungeon. You may find heated swimming pools, lighted tennis courts, indoor and outdoor tracks, squash, racketball, and paddleball courts, courts for volleyball and basketball, fields for football, lacrosse, and soccer. There may be Nautilus equipment, exercycles, trampolines, saunas, and whirlpools. Activities range from folk dancing, to martial arts, to whitewater rafting, to intramural sports. Find for yourself whatever you need to blow off steam and keep yourself fit. College is a great time in your life to start a healthy life style.

Ombudsman

Several hundred colleges have an ombudsman. If you've got a grievance, this is the person to see. He can tell you what the appropriate channels are, who you should talk to, what your rights are, what you should say, and what forms you need to fill out. Unfair treatment by a professor, administrator, or agency is a typical problem that an ombudsman can help you solve. If your school doesn't have one, your Dean of Students is probably your next best bet.

SPECIAL RESOURCES FOR SPECIAL NEEDS

Colleges today serve many more kinds of students than they have in the past. There are more women. More students come from ethnic and racial minorities. Many students are over the age of twenty-five. There are also commuters, married students, single parents, physically handicapped and learning disabled students, and part-time students who are employed, to name a few. Whatever your unique situation, take advantage of your resources. Here are a few campus agencies that serve different types of students.

Resources For Nontraditional Students

You're older and may have a family. Many of you work, some of you, full-time. Most of you commute to your campus. You might be changing your career in mid-life, or you might be a displaced homemaker. You could be a veteran or a mother whose children are all finally in school. You have different sets of needs and problems, but you all have one thing in common. You're different than the young adult just out of high school. You've seen more of life, you're more mature, you're concerned with different issues.

Your differences from "mainstream" students may leave you feeling out of place on campus. What could you have to talk about with students whose interests seem bounded by new-wave music and football weekends? In spite of impressive achievements, many of you lack confidence in your scholastic abilities. It's understandable if you haven't taken a test in ten or twenty years. Your additional responsibilities often take time and energy away from studies. If you're a single parent of two who works twenty-five hours a week and takes three classes, you must juggle an incredible number of tasks every day.

We have devoted an entire chapter of this book to organizational skills. They are doubly important for nontraditional students. Budgeting your time effectively is an absolute must.

The other key to your success is to develop a support system. The difficulty in doing so is that organized campus resources have historically been designed for young adults who live on campus. The counseling center may close at 5:00 P.M.—which might be the earliest time you could use it. Happily, colleges are beginning to respond to the greater numbers of nontraditional students. More agencies, programs, and facilities are available during weekends and evening hours, and others are being designed for your needs. If your school is dragging its feet in this area, inform the administration.

It is vital that you know just what is available. The trouble is, you may be so busy that you hardly have time to find out. In many cases there are special orientation sessions for returning students. If not, make every effort to attend the regular orientation, even if you have to take vacation or sick leave to do it. Does your college provide day-care? If not, is there a community day-care service with a sliding scale? Can single parents live in married student housing? Is there a university ombudsman to help cut through red tape and listen to your grievances. Does the counseling center offer any program specifically suited to your situation?

Don't limit your support to administrators and counselors. It is a serious handicap not to know other students. How else will you get notes and assignments when you miss a class? Try to meet others who share your concerns. You can work out car pools, baby sitting co-ops, and study groups. Often there are support groups for single parents, reentry homemakers, and the like. You may need to organize a group if one doesn't already exist. Talk with your dean. of students. Take out an ad in the school newspaper. If you want to be a blue-chipper, you can't sit on your hands and wait to be rescued— you've got to take action.

If you're married, be very clear about the mutual expectations of you and your spouse. Will your spouse have to assume more financial or homemaking responsibilities? It's best to try and iron out such questions ahead of time. There are few burdens heavier than a resentful mate. Conversely, a truly supportive partner can make all the difference in the world.

Resources for the Physically/Learning Disabled

Some individuals prefer the term "handicapped"; others prefer "disabled." Whichever you choose, there are more of you succeeding in college than ever before. The federal government has set up guidelines to ensure that colleges and universities are accessible to you. High-tech products, specifically designed for the disabled, have made adjustment to college easier. Faculty and staff are learning to be supportive without being patronizing. All of these factors help validate your conviction that you can lead a full life in spite of being dyslexic or being confined to a wheelchair.

Colleges are becoming more sensitive to the impact of the environment on the physically disabled. Rampways, handrails, and elevators make the campus more manageable. In some institutions special transportation is available. On many campuses, such as the University of Nebraska at Lincoln, specially equipped dorm rooms are available. Other schools will provide attendants, some of them live-in, for little or no cost.

The latest equipment is mind-boggling. Typewriters that transpose into braille, readers that magnify or accept braille input, and Kurzweil reading machines are just a few of these wonders. The Kurzweil device can view any printed material, regardless of the language, and read it out loud.

The College Guide For Students With Disabilities provides information about services and facilities on different campuses. If your school can't meet all your needs, there are a number of nonprofit groups that may take up the slack. For example, there is a national service organization that will record any educational book free of charge for anyone who cannot read standard printed material because of a disability (contact RECORDING FOR THE BLIND, The Anne T. Macdonald Center, 20 Roszel Road, Princeton, NJ 08540, 609/452-0606).

If you have a learning disability, you need encouragement and support. Because your disability isn't obvious, it may be difficult for others to understand your particular needs. Happily, many campuses provide specialists who work hard to give you, the LD student, a positive college experience.

Most established programs offer some of the following types of assistance: diagnostic testing and prescriptive planning, academic program advisement, psychological and career counseling, remedial programs, tutoring, and special course offerings. Other services and aids include typewriters, word processors, notetakers, alternative test arrangements, advocacy, and special housing.

There are approximately 380 four-year colleges and universities that will accept students with learning disabilities. More than 250 schools offer full-service programs. Ohio State serves over four hundred students. At this time DeSisto College in Florida is the only school in the nation that offers a complete curriculum for learning disabled students. For more information take a look at *Lovejoy's College Guide For The Learning Disabled*, by Charles Straughn II and Dr. Marvelle Colby.

Resources For Racial And Ethnic Minorities

Our comments in the next several paragraphs are based on the experience of black students attending predominantly white colleges. Blacks are not the only group who have suffered from discrimination and oppression, however. Hispanics and native Americans have also been treated unfairly at one time or another, as have members of just about every other racial, religious, or culturally different group you can think of. So this section applies to anyone who has suffered by virtue of his or her minority status.

With the end of legally segregated education in 1954, blacks have attended predominantly white colleges in increasing numbers. Their rate of graduation, unfortunately, has lagged behind their rate of admission. Scholars give several reasons for this lower rate of success.

First, there is the simple fact of being in the minority and feeling out of place. For most of you, there is culture shock. For many of you, it is extreme. The fashions, musical tastes, and customs that you grew up with are suddenly rare or altogether absent. Everything seems a little strange. You're no longer sure what to say or how to act. All of this can bewilder you and shake your confidence.

For some of you, even the language is different. "Black English" may be a legitimate subject of inquiry for scholars, but its use on a term paper will result in a loss of credit.

Who do you socialize with? Who do you date? These are very important issues, particularly for young adults. If you're one of a handful of blacks, your choices are very limited. It's common for blacks to feel lonely and isolated on a white campus.

For a number of blacks there is a legacy of oppression to overcome. You are less likely to have college-educated parents. Your high school may have lacked resources. And when you look around the campus, you see precious few black faculty and administrators to symbolize the fact that you can make it.

Another factor is that racism has not been completely eliminated. While it is rarely blatantly oppressive, its presence in subtle forms can still be destructive. Faculty may have lower expectations of you. Other students may interpret your cultural differences in a negative light. The curriculum tends to be "white": Teachers and textbooks seldom mention black contributions to science, letters, politics or the arts.

So, in the face of all this, how can blacks (or any other minority) succeed? You succeed first the same way anyone else does—by being goal-directed and hardworking and smart. The principles underlying the Blue-Chip Master Plan apply to everyone. But because of the difficulties cited above, it is especially important that blacks make use of campus resources.

You should seek out any black faculty and staff on your campus. These are the ones who have made it. Here are role models and potential mentors. Similarly, as an incoming black student, you should identify the black upperclassmen who are achievers. They can provide information and support and show you the ropes. Many schools have a special agency for blacks or minorities. It is important that you take advantage of this resource. Here you can learn more about your cultural heritage, form friendships, and find programs to meet your particular needs. Finally, you must resist the awkwardness your minority status may elicit and actively use all the campus resources that are available. The same applies to forming friendships and professional relationships with all members of your campus community. If you want to succeed in a salad-bowl society—

one that is made up of many different races and cultures, each retaining its own identity—you must be able to relate effectively to all kinds of people.

We have worked with a number of blue-chip blacks. As their number grows, we hope they will give a new and happier twist to the old lyric, "Why am I so black and blue?"

Resources For Women

In the 1970s women on campus were demanding their own services. In 1986, with more women succeeding in the professions and in managerial positions, the trend is to farm these services out to other campus agencies. Check with the Office of Student Services to find out exactly what is available.

A few universities, such as the University System in California, continue to provide women's centers for their female students. Most coeducational schools employ female counselors and gynecologists. Many colleges sponsor ongoing programs or short seminars designed for females. Topics include discrimination in the workplace, the battered woman, the displaced homemaker, assertiveness/leadership training, date-rape, and career assistance for those interested in nontraditional fields.

Most schools offer some sort of self-defense training, whether through the physical education department or the Counseling Center. And most schools will provide nighttime escorts and/or shuttle services. On many urban campuses you would be well advised to use them.

If your school doesn't have what you need and you're interested in starting a program, there are several things you can do. Talk to someone in student government. Talk to someone in the office of student services. If funding is a problem, look into off-campus money. *Grants For Women And Girls* is an excellent reference book put out by the Foundation Center in New York City. It is the grants research tool most widely used by fundraisers for female programs (see "More To Read" in the Appendices for a complete address).

SUMMARY

1. Everybody needs to ask for help at times.
2. Blue-chippers never hesitate to seek help when they need it.
3. Blue-chippers make a point to become familiar with the resources available to them.
4. College campuses are filled with sources of help in all areas of students' lives. Most services are free or available at minimal cost.
5. Support services are especially important for nontraditional, physically or learning disabled, and minority students.
6. Learning to recognize those times when you need help and knowing where to find it are two important steps in becoming a blue-chipper in college and throughout life.

11
What Makes Achievers Tick?

Blue-chippers are achievers, but what makes them go? Great tomes have been written on the psychology of achievement. We believe all this material can be boiled down to one short sentence: Achievers are goal directed. Goal and *Direction*. Let's take a look at each.

GOALS

1. *Achievers set goals.* They aim for excellence: building a better "widget," writing an *A* term paper, instilling a love of learning in first-graders.

2. *Achievers set **clear** goals.* There is a big difference between dreams and plans. Anyone can fantasize about fame and fortune, but a plan requires concrete, specific objectives to shoot for. Blue-chippers take the trouble to make their goals clear. Too many students say, "I'm going to get a lot of studying done this weekend," or "I want to make it big in High Tech." Blue-chippers say, "I'm going to study history for two hours Saturday morning and work math problems for two hours on Sunday afternoon," or "I'm going to major in electrical engineering so I can eventually develop computer hardware." When you set clear goals, you can tell whether you're really making progress. If you are, success is a powerful motivator. If not,

you can adjust your plans.

3. *Achievers set **realistic** goals.* Their goals demand talent and effort, but they are do-able. Blue-chippers don't take long shots. They don't depend on luck. Achievers like a challenge with some risk, but not the probability of failure.

One way psychologists have studied achievement is to watch subjects compete at a ring-toss game. If points are awarded based on distance from the target, players who throw from medium range almost always win the most points. They also reveal the highest drive for success on other measures. And, most importantly, they tend to be the best students, the most effective salespeople, the most successful entrepreneurs.

Underachievers go after ridiculously easy goals or impossibly hard ones. Blue-chippers like a challenge, but they don't want to be overwhelmed. They aim for the middle. Then, as soon as they reach their goals of moderate difficulty, they set their sights one notch higher.

4. *Achievers set long-term, intermediate, and short-term goals.* Successful entrepreneurs often have five-year plans, quarterly goals, and a weekly calendar. Blue-chip students operate similarly. The Four-Year Master Plan (Appendix I) is an example of long-term and medium-range objectives. The section on time management in Chapter 3 covers all three types of goals.

DIRECTION

Direction implies action, movement, getting things done, making things happen. The director of a movie, more than anyone else, determines the quality of the film. A director is in charge.

Achievers are also in charge. They don't wait passively for success to come their way. They strive to reach their goals. Here's how:

1. *Achievers think a lot about their goals and how to reach them.* They daydream about them, juggling strategies and weighing alternatives. Since they think about how to reach their goals so much of the time, they come up with a lot of shortcuts, improvements, and better methods.

Just about everybody dreams of success. Blue-chippers go one step farther—they dream how to make it happen!

2. *Achievers plan.* They're more time conscious. They set objec-

tives and deadlines on paper—and keep score of how they're doing. This is why we urge blue-chippers to use daily to-do lists and to map out their assignments for an entire semester.

3. *Achievers prioritize.* Working hard and getting lots of things done may not be enough if you neglect something important. It's getting the most important things done that makes someone a blue-chipper.

4. *Achievers take it step by step.* They implement the good plans they make. They break up large tasks into smaller ones. A year-long project can be divided into a series of shorter deadlines. A college education can be divided into four years, each year into semesters, each semester into weeks. A term paper can be similarly chopped up into manageable tasks.

5. *Achievers overcome barriers.* When they run into roadblocks, they keep trying till they find a way to get around them. Naturally, they can get discouraged too, but they bounce back from defeat rather than letting it keep them down. If personal shortcomings hold them back, they find a way to compensate or they change. They never wait to be rescued. They actively seek out expert help whenever it's needed to get the job done.

One of our greatest satisfactions is watching college students develop. We've seen country bumpkins overcome their lack of sophistication. We've seen shy students join clubs so they can learn to conduct a meeting. We've known pre-meds who managed to eke out *B*s in calculus because they studied overtime and hired a tutor.

Blue-chippers come in all sizes and shapes. One thing they have in common is that they don't easily take "no" for an answer. They're not quick to throw in the towel. They encounter their share of setbacks, but they keep on keeping on.

We recall one young woman from a rural background whose father had died when she was a child. Her mother discouraged her from applying to a competitive college. She filled out the forms by herself and also applied for financial aid. When she arrived on campus, she felt out of place, and she had to struggle to survive in class. Her boyfriend kept after her to transfer to the junior college in her hometown. Besides, who needed a college degree? She could always clerk in the local dime store.

With some difficulty, she broke things off with her old boyfriend. She joined a study group, and that helped her with her grades. She got counseling to improve her self-confidence. She had to work part-time to make ends meet. At first, she waited tables, but eventually she did drafting for a small engineering company. She finally managed to graduate and began working full-time for the same firm.

It wasn't a very good job. Her attempts at finding a better one didn't lead to much, so she got help from her college's career planning center. She developed a better job search plan and improved her resume. She was discouraged to discover she was no longer eligible to set up interviews through the campus placement center. But she didn't give up. She began dropping by the placement office at noon and started having lunch with corporate recruiters. Within a few months she had been invited to interview with several companies. She received several offers and accepted the one she felt was best for her.

We are proud to know this woman who was born into near poverty. Her family and friends advised her against pursuing her dreams. She made mistakes, and she encountered innumerable barriers to success. But she didn't give up.

Today, she is an engineer for a Fortune 500 corporation. She designs radar systems for supersonic aircraft.

IT'S ALL UP TO YOU

If you want success you've got to believe it's up to you to go out and get it.

Who determines your destiny? You? Or is your future controlled by forces outside yourself? Your answers to these questions have a powerful affect on what you accomplish. If you believe you control your future, psychologists say you have an internal "locus of control." If you believe you're a passive victim to what fate brings, they say you possess an external "locus of control."

We believe the foundation of all achievement lies in believing that planning and effort can influence the future. So, are you the kind of person who lays plans to open a business in five years? Or do you figure, "Why bother? Something will go wrong. It always does." Can you pass up the *Monday Night Movie* in order to fine tune your resume? Or do you think, "It's not worth it. You've got to have connections to work for that company." Do you study harder after a bad grade? Or do you say, "It doesn't do any good to prepare for that teacher's tests anyway."

HOW TO GET MORE GO

Chances are, you believe you can strongly influence your own future. You probably are the kind of person who is motivated to achieve or you wouldn't have read this far. But suppose you're not. You might be reading this chapter because it's required for a course. And now you're convinced that you're very externally oriented and have very little in common with achievers. Well, don't despair. You can change.

In 1959, psychologist George Burris taught underachieving college students some of the same principles we've outlined in this chapter. In just one semester he got results. Achievement motivation scores went up, and so did grades. Another psychologist, Robert DeCharms, worked with teachers of disadvantaged children. He emphasized their working to develop an internal locus of control in the students. And the students' grades improved significantly.

DeCharms has developed an innovative way of thinking about power and achievement. He says people tend to be either pawns or origins. Pawns are passive, generally acted upon, and don't have much control over their future. Origins, on the other hand, actively determine what happens to them.

You can take the pawn analogy one step further—individuals can be compared to the pieces in a game of chess. A pawn is the least powerful piece. Basically, a pawn can move straight ahead, one square at a time. It enjoys very little choice or power. When confronted with an obstacle, it can only wait until the obstacle is removed.

If, however, a pawn is passed all the way to the end of the board, it can be exchanged for a queen. A queen can move vertically, horizontally, or diagonally. It can go forward or backward for as many squares as there are on the board. Talk about controlling your own destiny! The queen has the whole board to play with. The pawn has just one square.

Suppose a queen mistakenly thought she was a pawn. Her choices would be drastically limited. Conversely, if a pawn started acting like a queen, the sky would be the limit.

Why do some people become pawns and others queens? Why do some students feel powerless to influence their futures, while others are convinced their efforts can make a difference?

Any kind of oppression undermines the development of motivation. Oppression can be blatant, like racism or poverty. It can be as subtle as overprotective parents. But it's too late to change where you grew up or how your parents raised you.

So what can you do if you want to achieve more? First, as simple as it sounds, you've got to believe that your own efforts make a difference.

If we haven't convinced you, please talk to a counselor. Virtually all counselors are committed to helping their clients become more independent, more in charge of their own lives.

Second, follow the suggestions in this book. We didn't pull them out of a hat. Our ideas come directly from the experts on achievement motivation, such as Harvard's David McClelland. Look at the Table of Contents. Every chapter has to do with planning, organizing, developing skills, using resources, and setting goals.

Psychologist Martin Seligman has studied helplessness in animals and humans. He finds that subjects can be trained to be helpless by exposing them to insoluble problems. When they're faced with different problems—ones that do have a solution—they *don't bother to try*. If you believe you can't succeed, you *can't*. The only thing that seems to change helpless individuals is to make them act constructively. Eventually they see that their efforts do make a difference.

We can't make you follow our suggestions. But we urge you to try them. They work. Your performance will improve. You'll taste success.

And success breeds success.

We guarantee it.

Here's a way to assess your own blue-chip achievement motivation.

QUICK-SCORING ACHIEVEMENT MOTIVATION QUIZ

Points   Score

1. <u>0</u> I have no clear goals in life.
   <u>1</u> I have a general idea of a career in which I want to succeed.
   <u>2</u> I set daily objectives which advance me toward my long-term goals.
   <u>3</u> I set daily, weekly, and quarterly goals which will advance me toward my long-term goals.   _____

2. <u>0</u> I'm too proud to accept help, no matter how stuck or lost I get.
   <u>1</u> I will accept help, but only when it's offered.
   <u>2</u> I actively seek out expert help whenever I get stuck or lost.
   <u>3</u> I am acquainted with most campus resources and regularly use them without becoming dependent upon them.   _____

3. <u>0</u> I tend to give up after the first setback.
   <u>1</u> I eventually bounce back from a setback after a period of immobilization.
   <u>2</u> I analyze my setbacks instead of kicking myself or blaming others.
   <u>3</u> A setback inspires me to try again, using new methods if needed.   _____

4. <u>0</u> My fantasies about career success are limited to scenes from *Lifestyles of the Rich & Famous.*
   <u>1</u> My fantasies about career success include practical details of my future world of work.
   <u>2</u> My fantasies about career success include thinking about practical steps I can take on a daily basis.
   <u>3</u> My fantasies about career success include long-range, intermediate, and daily plans to reach my goals.   _____

5. <u>0</u> Most of my goals are so high that I seldom reach them or so low that I reach them with very little effort.

<u>1</u>   At least some of my goals are moderately difficult—
      high enough to challenge me but low enough not
      to overwhelm me with anxiety.
<u>2</u>   Most of my goals are moderately difficult.
<u>3</u>   Most of my goals are moderately difficult, and
      increase their difficulty as I reach them.   _____

Scoring:
0   Points —   If you don't crawl out from under the doormat
                   and join the human race, you have about as much
                   chance at success as a slug with a lobotomy.

1-5   Points —   The beginning stages of the blue-chip mindset are
                   showing. Still a ways to go though.

6-10   Points —   You're on the way, but watch out—success can be
                   addictive.

11-15   Points —   Blue-chip material. You can turn your dreams
                   into reality.

12

Doctor, Lawyer, Chief Executive Officer: The Sequel

Once you finish your junior year, you'll be faced with some important decisions. Should you begin working after graduation or start on an advanced degree? Although there are twelve months before you graduate, you should start refining you goals now. Many corporations recruit heavily in the fall. Graduate and professional schools have February application deadlines. What's your next step?

CLARIFYING YOUR GOALS: THE NEVER-ENDING STORY

You have to know yourself and the job world before you can make sound career decisions. You've already chosen a major and a general career direction. Now it's time to get more specific. As a blue-chipper, checking your goals is an ongoing, lifelong process.

Graduate School

Will graduate school help you reach your goals? This is the first question you must answer before you seriously consider applying. If it's your next step because you don't know what else to do, chances are good you'il be in the same boat when you get your advanced degree. There are plenty of PhDs driving cabs and typing memos.

For openers, read Appendix V, "Should I Get An Advanced

Degree?" Then start asking people who should know. Counselors and placement workers can give you some advice. So can your professors. But don't fail to ask people in your chosen field. If you want to be a research engineer, the best person to ask about the marketability of an advanced degree is another research engineer or somebody who hires them.

Some companies prefer to do their own training. They believe that they can better teach new employees how specifically to meet the needs of the company than can a graduate school. On the other hand, more than a few corporations will help you get an advanced degree, provided you agree to continue working for them. They want a return on their investment. MBAs are very popular these days. We think they make the most sense after you've worked for a few years.

If you go to graduate school, it's important to find the program that's right for you. Factors to consider include cost, location, degree requirement, courses, and reputation. The reputation of a school is determined by the quality of the faculty, the library, and the research facilities. The *Gourman Report* rates the top schools in each field. Try to find a school whose philosophy is congenial with yours. A very good school might have a theoretical orientation, and if you want application, you'll be out of luck.

OK, suppose an advanced degree will help you reach your goals. In some cases it's a requirement—law, medicine, and college teaching come to mind. Can you get accepted, and will you be able to do the work?

Most graduate programs admit on the basis of grades and admissions tests such as the GRE, the Miller Analogies Test, and the Medical College Admission Test. Do some research at the library or counseling center. Find out what the requirements are. Pace's, Peterson's, and Barron's all publish reliable guides to graduate and professional programs. If your preliminary research is encouraging, you can find out more specific information from the catalog of the school in question. Your professors all went to grad school, so be sure and check with them. Should you decide to apply, you will need letters of recommendation from some of them.

Your SAT scores are pretty good predictors of what you'll make on the GRE or the MCAT. If you don't do well on standardized tests, there are study guides and courses available to help you improve your scores.

Once you get into a graduate program, your chances are good that you'll complete it. Graduate education is very expensive, and schools don't like to flunk their students out. About 98 percent of all medical students get their M.D. The same blue-chip character traits that produce success in college will help you get an advanced degree— working hard in an organized way toward clear, realistic goals. Graduate work requires much more independent study. There are fewer tests and papers, but they are bigger and each one counts for more. Many degrees require theses or dissertations.

GOODBYE IVORY TOWER— HELLO, REAL WORLD

Most of you will want to begin full-time employment shortly after your bachelor's degree. And you'll want to have a good job lined up and waiting for you long before you get your diploma. That means you'll be conducting a job search at the same time you're completing your senior year. To do this right you've got to know yourself. You can't market yourself if you don't know what you have to offer.

One way to assess your skills is to think of every job, school project, or extracurricular activity as being a series of lesser tasks (which, by the way, they are). If you further reduce the different tasks, you have a list of skills needed to do them.

For example, one student doing a social work internship participated in the development of a geriatric day-care center. Her tasks involved: assessing the needs of the target population; developing a suitable recreational program; scheduling activities; and coordinating transportation for participants.

These tasks required the following skills to do the job: communication; organizational ability; creativity; analytical ability.

She was then able to use these skills in marketing herself to employers. If you're still stuck, try the exercise at the conclusion of this chapter.

Employers want to know what you can do for them, and they need to know quickly. Corporate recruiters scan hundreds of resumes and interview dozens of prospects every week. How can you show them what you've got in language they understand?

THE STAR TECHNIQUE

Virtually all jobs consist of problems waiting to be solved. You need to show employers how you can help solve their problems. If you have the right skills, you can do this. The STAR Technique is a method for identifying your skills and communicating them to those in a position to hire you.

STAR TECHNIQUE

Your skills—what you can actually DO for an employer—are potentially your strongest selling points. But don't just list them. Give examples to show *how* you are skilled at XYZ. Be descriptive and use action words.

You can strengthen an example by including an outcome. If you quantify (e.g., *20%* increase) the results, your example will have even more punch. Sometimes you can't readily quantify results; you have to imply them (e.g, familiarity with different computer languages implies proficiency in them.) If possible, include a positive outcome (e.g., *successfully* implemented new budgeting procedure). Remember, positive results create positive reactions.

Use the STAR (Situation—Action—Result) TECHNIQUE which is frequently used in personnel work, to communicate your skills with impact.

ST ....SITUATION ....WHAT
                                   OCCURRED

A ....ACTION ....HOW IT WAS
                                   HANDLED

R ....RESULT(S) ....THE OUTCOME

Examples of skills using the STAR TECHNIQUE
* Successfully organized parents' group at Day-Care Center
* Conversant in French, Spanish, and German
* Wrote four competitive contract proposals that were success-fully funded for approximately ½-million dollars each
* Developed marketing strategy for new product which sur-passed sales of previous product by 50%
* Managed Pizza Hut Restaurant with annual revenue of one million dollars, annual payroll of ¼-million dollars
* Implemented student-centered teaching to 5th-grade class that resulted in average increase in student achievement-test scores of 17%
* Handled public relations for benefit concert in civic center resulting in first sellout in 7-year history of the event

---

Employers have to deal with the real world of limited resources, fierce competition, and the bottom line. They're used to thinking in terms of practical problems, the action taken, and what the conse-quences are. A salesman takes on a slumping territory, talks to plant managers instead of office managers and doubles orders in six months. A design engineer introduces computer-assisted design to a project and beats the deadline by two months. A manager introduces an incentive program for her staff, and absenteeism is halved, saving the company $500,000 annually.

Employers want results, preferably quantifiable results. More dol-lars earned. Fewer hours taken. A greater percent of the market. Better achievement-test scores from the students.

You probably haven't made anybody megabucks yet, but the same principles apply at any age. A twelve-year-old gets more subscrip-tions on his paper route than any other carrier and wins a new bike. A high-school student organizes a lawn-care business and builds a clientel of sixty-five regular customers. A college freshman makes an *A* in Computer Science and learns FORTRAN and BASIC. A co-op student assists in developing a system of inventory control that gets the product to the customer three days faster than her company's leading competitor. A fraternity pledge trainer raises the pledges' grades by an average of four-tenths of a point, and for the first time in the organization's history an entire pledge class is initiated on time.

You can't just tell prospective employers that you have salesmanship, entrepreneurial know-how, computer skills, organizational ability, and leadership (which are the five skills implied in the paragraph above). You've got to show them. The STAR Technique enables you to do just that. We believe your skills should be the focus of your entire job-search campaign. You will highlight them on your resume, emphasize them during interviews, mention them in your correspondence.

The ability to convey your marketable skills concisely, with impact, is itself an impressive skill. Think about it. You demonstrate analytical ability, communications skills, self-awareness, and organizational skills—a not-too-shabby list of selling points to have working for you everytime you contact an employer.

Once you come up with your marketable skills via the STAR Technique, you've completed the most difficult phase of the job search. And since you have identified what you've got going for yourself, you'll also feel like a million dollars. We think that's a pretty good way to start any important endeavor.

If you get stuck, use the exercise following the summary to unstick you.

SUMMARY

1. Start making your post-graduation plans at the end of your junior year.
2. Clarifying your goals is an ongoing process.
3. Determine if graduate school will help you meet your goals.
4. Assess your marketable skills.
5. The STAR Technique is a powerful tool for analyzing your strengths and conveying them to others.

DEFINING SKILLS IN LIFE EXPERIENCES

WORK HISTORY

Job Titles   Main Duties

Work Responsibilities Most Liked   Why?

Work Responsibilities Least Liked   Why?

What skills and abilities did you utilize
in your preferred work responsibilities?

VOLUNTEER WORK HISTORY

Job Titles   Main Duties

Work Responsibilities Most Liked   Why?

Work Responsibilities Least Liked   Why?

What skills and abilities did you utilize
in your preferred work responsibilities?

ORGANIZATION WORK HISTORY

Position Titles   Main Duties

Work Responsibilities Most Liked   Why?

Work Responsibilities Least Liked   Why?

What skills and abilities did you utilize
in your preferred work responsibilities?

COURSEWORK	
Courses	Description
Coursework Most Liked	Why?
Coursework Least Liked	Why?

What skills and abilities did you utilize
in your preferred coursework?

HOBBIES AND LEISURE PURSUITS

Activities   Description

Activities Most Liked   Why?

Activities Least Liked   Why?

What skills and abilities did you utilize
in your preferred activities?

SKILLS DEFINITION

Based on this exercise, list all skills and abilities that you
have defined. After your list has been compiled, circle the
FIVE MOST IMPORTANT skills and abilities. This
inventory will be a helpful tool in creating your job objective for your resume.

13
It's A Jungle Out There— The Job Search

We have some good news and some bad. College graduates might not have to fight quite as hard as they did between 1975 and 1985. The Baby Boom generation has passed the baton to its children, and there are fewer of you. The U.S. Bureau of Labor estimates that through 1995 approximately 850,000 students will graduate annually. During this same period there will be about 675,000 job openings for college graduates each year.

Between 1984 and 1995 the number of jobs requiring at least a bachelor's degree will increase by 45 percent. That's three times more than the 15 percent growth projected for all jobs. Eight out of nine college grads will get jobs requiring a degree. That's the good news.

The bad news is that employers will continue the current trend of educational upgrading—hiring college graduates to perform jobs previously filled by people with less education. When you think about it, it's inevitable. International competition has forced American business and industry to be more selective about whom they hire. Besides, with a higher percentage of degreed candidates to choose from, companies can require a higher level of education of their new employees. Unfortunately, these upgraded positions don't necessarily mean upgraded salaries or more opportunities for advancement.

But what's a graduate to do? A mediocre job beats another year of peanut butter-and-jelly sandwiches or bunking with your kid brother again. The 1984-1985 *Occupational Outlook Handbook* reported that during the seventies about one of five college graduates felt significantly underemployed.

You wouldn't be reading this book if you didn't want to improve your chances for success. Each chapter outlines a different phase of an overall strategy for reaching your goals. By working harder and smarter than the average student, you make an investment in your future. You develop yourself into a blue-chip graduate.

But there's one last hurdle—you've got to understand how the job search works. Not only must you be a blue-chipper. You've got to find a blue-chip job. And then you've got to convince someone that you can fill it.

GETTING STARTED

The Want Ads

It seems like a reasonable place to begin until you reflect on it. Companies will fill many vacant positions by promoting from within their own organization, by shifting employees laterally, or by locating a strong candidate through the "grapevine." The jobs that remain find their way into the want ads. They are not usually the most desirable jobs.

On top of that, jobs are sometimes advertised after they are already filled. This is so the company will appear to comply with government guidelines for fair hiring practices. Richard Bolles says that about twenty-four out of one hundred job seekers get jobs through the want ads. So it's one place to look, but don't confine yourself to the newspapers.

Our guess is that ads placed in trade journals are more likely to point to good jobs. If a company took the trouble to place the ad, they're probably serious. On the other hand, more time has elapsed, so the job may already be filled.

Employment Agencies

Bolles claims about twenty-four succeed using this route too. The bottom line on employment agencies is that they are paid a commission to get a job filled. They will work the hardest for applicants who have the greatest chance of being hired. It is not cost effective for them to do extensive counseling. They are turned off by the person who wanders in and says, "I have a degree in X. Find me a job." They want to work with people who have done some serious self-assessment and know what they have to offer.

If you use an employment agency, treat your first meeting like a screening interview because that's exactly what it is. They're deciding if you're worth spending their time on. Take your resume. Practice the STAR technique. Use interviewing etiquette—proper dress, positive attitude, enthusiasm, etc. Be familiar with Chapters 12 (self-assessment), 14 (resume), and 15 (interviewing) of this book before you start.

College Placement Offices

There is no guarantee of a blue-chip job here either, but your success depends in large measure on the particular university and its placement center. As we mentioned earlier, one way employers have cut expenses is by recruiting at fewer colleges.

Placement is a student service, so by all means take advantage of it. Here are some hints to help you get the best results:

1. Sign up early. Don't wait until the last minute on any aspect of the job search.
2. Attend the orientation session(s). Comply fully with the established rules and procedures of the placement office. If you don't, you may hurt your chances for getting interviews with your preferred companies.
3. Get a list of which employers will be visiting your campus. Identify which of those companies you would like to work for. Establish a group of favorite companies and another group of acceptable alternatives.
4. Prepare your personal resume(s), data sheets, applications, etc. DON'T SKIMP. Do it right (see Chapter 14).

There is no standard way for a placement center to assign interviews. Some use a lottery. In some centers the companies are given access to student resumes and data sheets. The companies grant interviews only to those students whose records catch their eye.

If at first you don't get an interview with a company you're keen on, don't give up. Put your resume with a strong cover letter in the company's message slot while their representative is on campus. Tell them why you think you match their needs and request an interview. Another alternative is to show up personally at the placement center on a day when the company's recruiter will be there, but during a time when he or she won't actually be meeting with students—early in the morning, at lunch time, or near the end of the day. Ask for an impromptu interview. The worst that can happen is that your request will be declined.

If your major is not highly recruited, check with your academic department. Your professors may have some job leads, and in some instances placement may be handled at the departmental level.

Join a professional association relevant to your professional goals. Sometimes they will have placement services for members. If you need information about such organizations, look in *The Encyclopedia Of Associations*, which is found in most main libraries. Even more important than any formalized placement assistance, professional associations are excellent sources of contacts and information. Which brings us to our final method of finding a job.

Networking

Bolles says networking is *the* way to fly. He reports an 85 percent success rate. Rather better, wouldn't you say, than the one in 1,499 chance he reports for those who launch a blind resume campaign by mail.

If you've followed the Master Plan, you should have developed a network of professional contacts by now. If you feel deficient in this important blue-chip area, review Chapter 8.

Contacts can come from anywhere. Professors and employers are obvious choices, but also consider calling on family connections, friends who have already joined the work force, alumni from your hometown or from the town where you want to work. If you haven't already done so, join a professional association and start attending their meetings.

If it was smart to file your contacts as a sophomore, it's absolutely essential that you be organized now. We recommend a three-by-five card file system. On the front of each card put the name, address, phone number, and the person's position. Also indicate your referral source as that will help you make the proper approach. On the back put the dates when you meet and the nature of the conversation.

This is also a time when it is especially important to keep your calendar up to date. Immediately enter the time of every meeting you set—you don't want to miss any.

Bear in mind that when you're networking for jobs, you're not actually applying for work. You're trying to find out about your field. You're looking for leads. You're wanting feedback on your qualifications and credentials. Naturally, you wouldn't turn down a good job offer, but networking doesn't usually get you a job by tomorrow or even next week. But if you keep after it for several months, you should have a number of offers to consider. You'll also have contacts who can help you throughout your career.

APPROACHING THE CONTACT

If you write a letter, you can say clearly what needs to be said without distraction. The mail is slower, of course, than the phone, and your letter may be screened. The prospective contact may never lay eyes on it. In any event, you'll probably have to follow up your letter with a phone call to set up a meeting.

The main difficulty with phoning your contact is getting through. Part of a secretary's job is to protect her boss, so you may get put off. Here are some tips to help you reach the contact:

1. Phone after five. The secretary's having drinks at a fern bar, but the executive is probably still in the office. Maybe he or she will pick up the phone after the twelfth ring.

2. Make the secretary your ally. Get her first and last name, and refer to her by her last name. Give her some respect, and she might give you some.

3. Don't volunteer information that can be used to screen you out. Be diplomatic but persistent — "Professor Jones referred me to Ms. Jackson, and I really need to speak to her personally."

4. If the contact is on another line, say that you'll be glad to hold.

5. Generally speaking, it's better to say you'll call back than to leave your name and number. Somehow or other, busy people never seem to return unsolicited phone calls.

Diane Thomas
Ivy Hall, Room 221
Vickery College
Vickery, VT 02345

Mr. Tom Jones, Vice-President
Public Relations
Dynamic Enterprises
300 Progress Avenue
Boston, MA 54321

March 1, 1987

Dear Mr. Jones:

Dr. Smith of the Communications Department at Vickery College
suggested that I contact you for information about Public Relations
work at the corporate level. I'm a Communications major who will
be graduating in two months. I completed an internship this past
summer with a small public relations firm in Smithville. I'm eager
to learn more about public relations work on a larger scale,
especially from someone whose firm's principle market is
teenagers. I will call you next week to see if you can fit me into
your busy schedule. Dr. Smith sends her warmest regards.

Sincerely,

Diane Thomas

Diane Thomas

When You Do Get Through

You must be ready. Know what you want. Know what you're going to say. This means thorough preparation before you make the call. We recommend having an outline of your intended comments at hand.

Introduce yourself by giving your name and referral source and stating the purpose of your call. Don't say you're looking for a job. Instead, tell the contact that you're about to graduate in _____ and you'd like to meet to talk about her area. Your experience and coursework have focused on _____, but you understand her area is rapidly expanding, and it's related to yours. Do your best to persuade the contact to meet you. Tell her you want to talk more about particular trends in her area. Identify them by name. If she's unwilling to meet with you, get as much information as you can on the telephone. If you keep trying, however, you will eventually find some qualified people who are willing to talk with you in person.

Meeting the Contact

Your purpose for meeting is to get information and advice. Review "Conducting an Informational Interview" in Chapter 5. One of the biggest mistakes you can make during such a meeting is to be vague and unfocused. So prepare thoroughly for the interview by researching the field or industry in question. Complete the self-assessment discussed in Chapter 12. Have a winning resume in hand (Chapter 14). Develop a new "industrial-strength" five-minute presentation. Remember, you're not a freshman any more. You're one step away from being a blue-chip graduate. Use the STAR Technique to highlight your key strengths.

Preparation is also one of the best antidotes to the jitters, so practice with a friend if you're still feeling nervous. Or talk to a tape recorder or a mirror.

When you finally meet the contact, remind her of your phone conversation and who suggested that you seek her counsel. Describe yourself to her via your five-minute presentation. That will help her advise you according to your specific situation. It's also an opportunity for you to sell yourself. While you didn't come to her for a job, you certainly wouldn't turn the right offer down.

Making an effective five-minute presentation is a skill that you can acquire with practice. It's not easy to give a thumbnail sketch of yourself that says something without its sounding like a canned speech. Try to strike a balance between being overly formal and speaking too conversationally. Try to relax, and remember: you're just one human being trying to tell another who you are so that the other's comments will be pertinent to your situation. You should also know that this is a commonly accepted business practice. It is unlikely that this is the first or last time your contact will hear such a presentation. You'll likely exchange pleasantries for a few minutes, but at some point it will be appropriate to tell your contact about yourself.

In Chapter 5, Janet Smith, freshman, conducted her first informational interview and made her first five-minute presentation. Now, as a senior, she's networking for job leads. Notice that this time she is more focused in her five-minute presentation. The same is true of her questions.

Five-Minute Presentation of Janet Smith, Senior

"I really appreciate your taking the time to talk with me about current trends in Industrial/Organizational Psychology. Dr. Schwartz said you were doing some really interesting training work with people in sales and middle management. First, let me tell you a little about myself.

"I'm a Psych major, and I'll be graduating at the end of the summer. I should have around a 3.3 grade point average, but I've made all As in my Psych classes except for one B in Physiological. I've done an internship at Acme Company under Dr. Score. Mostly I was involved in test construction. I wrote some of the items, helped with the item analysis, and interviewed most of the subjects.

"The thing was, I gradually realized that the interviewing portion of my job was giving me the most satisfaction. It's not that I didn't enjoy developing the tests themselves. It's just that I preferred having direct contact with people. One of the surveys we developed was designed specifically to assess the morale of people in sales. I could pretty well tell who was going to be successful based on the subjects' scores, but I wasn't supposed to say anything that would influence them. That part frustrated me. I really wanted to use the test results to help these people who were starting out in sales.

"I have done some training work already through my job as an area coordinator with the residence hall program. Before I could start out as a resident assistant, I had to learn basic communication skills and some crisis intervention techniques. This past fall I helped train the new crop of assistants. I consistently got very high ratings, both from the students and from the staff member from housing.

"So what I'm wondering is—How can I break into the training field? And is it possible to do this with only an undergraduate degree? What are my options, and what steps do I need to start taking?"

Basically, you're trying to find out through your questions how you can become more marketable. What specific skills should you try to strengthen? Do you need additional training or experience? While it's not appropriate to make a hard sell for yourself, do try to create interest in the mind of the contact whenever possible. For example, if she mentions the need for persuasive skills in her kind of position, recount a situation in which you were persuasive and ask her if that's the sort of ability she has in mind.

Ask her to react to your resume (see Chapter 14). What's missing? Is there any fluff that should be trimmed? And take this opportunity to expand your network. Could she suggest others in the field that you could talk with? Does she know of any leads for job openings. Thank her graciously, and offer her a copy of your resume for her files. Then thank her again in a letter.

Before you start arranging meetings with the new contacts she gave you, do some more homework. Revise your resume according to her suggestions. Read up on areas of deficiency that she uncovered. Or get some more training. After each round of interviews, try to strengthen your suitability for the requirements of the position you're investigating. If you're persistent, you will gradually become a stronger candidate in possession of a winning resume. And at some point you will get interviews for some attractive positions.

SUMMARY

1. The job market will remain relatively competitive for most college graduates through 1995, so use every avenue available to you.
2. The want ads and employment agencies are not generally highly effective avenues to blue-chip jobs.
3. The success rates of different college placement centers varies widely.
4. Follow your placement center's rules exactly to get maximum results.
5. If your placement center's success rate is low, networking is probably your best bet for finding a good job.
6. Start networking only after you've done your homework: self-assessment; a winning resume; preliminary research of field and position.

14
The Resume
(Packaging the
Blue-Chip Student)

If you're clear on your career goals and understand the job search process, writing a strong resume will be easy. Employers are looking for people who will solve their problems. All you have to do is show an employer that you're good at solving his kind of problem. Once you've convinced Dynamic Enterprises that you can meet their needs, you've created a match. You've also got a job offer on your hands.

The resume doesn't get you the job. The interview does that. But if your resume shows that you match the employer's needs, it will get you an interview. It is a graphic representation of who you are professionally. It's your personal ad.

First Impressions

For employers, the resume is a screening device. Big corporations get hundreds of thousands of them every year. You can pay an employment agency a hundred dollars to come up with a work of art on thirty weight paper, but it's still junk mail to the guy who has to read a hundred of them a day. So you've got ten, maybe twenty seconds to show him that your resume is worth a second look.

It's got to look "mahvelous." Which isn't all that hard to make happen. Use high quality eight and one-half by eleven inch paper—

white, off-white, light gray, or beige. Maybe a designer or entertainer could go with something flashier, but most job seekers are best served by a conservative, professional look.

Don't use the typewriter your grandfather used in 1937. Get hold of a good electric that types clean, or hire a professional typist. Better yet, put it on a floppy disk. (This is just one more instance where computer skills come in handy.) If you don't know word processing, any professional secretarial service will be able to do it for you. Don't run it off on a cheap dot-matrix printer. Having it printed looks great; but then you're locked into one generic resume, and that has some real disadvantages. We'll elaborate shortly. All you really need is a good original. You can have any number duplicated on high quality paper at a copy center.

Appearance, as well as content, tells the employer a lot about you. Your resume reflects the kind of work you're capable of producing. It should show that you're well organized, that you can communicate clearly, and that you can make a strong visual presentation. The acid test: Does it look good enough for prospective employers to send out as their own work? If it doesn't, it's not good enough.

Use some of the tricks that commercial artists use. When they design ads, they play up important information in the white space, those areas free from text. In poorly constructed resumes we often see dates in those big chunks of white space known as the margin. Dates *are not* selling points. Instead, use information that is: job titles, degrees, skills, etc.

Stay away from long paragraphs. Your resume should not look like a page out of your American history text. Ads use a few key words, carefully chosen and strategically placed. You further focus attention by using bold print, larger type, bullets or asterisks. Remember, you've got just ten seconds to get their attention.

The job objective is crucial because it informs the employer if there is a match. The job objective, unlike the rest of the resume, gets close attention on the first pass-through. Therefore, it comes immediately after your name and address at the top of the page. If you're offering what he's seeking, he'll read on.

RESUME FORMAT

		NAME			
Address	City	State		Zip	Phone

JOB OJECTIVE: Most important piece of information on resume; used by employers as screening device or to signal job match; must grab attention and motivate employer to read further (see handout on Job Objectives).

EDUCATION: List in reverse chronological order, putting the most promotable facts — school or degree — first.

Mention any outstanding honors or achievements, such as high GPA, Dean's List . . .

Give examples of relevant coursework and school-related activities if a recent graduate.

SKILLS:
- Choose skills that are most relevant to job objective.
- Give short statements to support skills.
- Make support statements results-oriented.
- Position most marketable skills first.

EMPLOYMENT: Place strongest of the two sections, employment or education first.

List in reverse chronological order, putting the most promotable facts — employer or job title — first.

Give functional description of job if employment history is strong and supports job objective.

MISCELLANEOUS:
- Call this section anything applicable — INTERESTS, ACTIVITIES, ACCOMPLISHMENTS, or ACHIEVEMENTS.
- Give only information that an employer would be interested in knowing.
- Stay away from personal and chatty information.

REFERENCE: Furnished upon request.

Remember: there are no concrete rules in resume preparation. Modify this guide, when necessary, to make the most favorable impression.

THE JOB OBJECTIVE

The following is a component sheet useful in developing a job objective. Pick the ones you feel are applicable to your situation.

- Include the exact job title if you know it. Do not guess! The job objective is used as a screening device. If you apply for a job that does not exist, your resume will probably be eliminated before it is read thoroughly. Don't chance it.

- Make the objective meaningful. Everything else in the resume must support and reflect what is said in the objective.

- Be specific and to the point. Broad objectives are often misinterpreted to be vague and uncertain. Avoid the use of platitudes and cliches. They say nothing and cast doubt on the rest of the resume.

- Include the field you were trained in if this is a selling point. This is especially applicable to those in technical fields.

- Include a sub-discipline if you have specialized in one. This will help to pinpoint where in the company you might be most useful.

- Include the functional area of the company where you want to work. Examples of these company divisions are: research and development, production, technical services, information systems/processing, marketing and sales, and administration and finance.

- Include skills/qualifications that are relevant to the job you are seeking. This will help promote you as a strong job candidate.

  Ex: Seek a position in civil engineering as a Structural Engineer utilizing my skills in structures, computer programming and construction.

- Include the type of organization if it is important to you. Keep in mind that this may limit the number of opportunities open to you.

- Note: If you have several different job objectives, you should have several different resumes.

Taking a Second Look

OK, she looked at your resume, and it looked good. Your career objective matches one of the positions she's filling. Now, she's willing to look more closely. And when she does, she *must* not see any misspelled words, typos, or grammatical errors. So proofread it carefully. Wait a day, and proof it again. Then let a friend take a look at it. Obviously, this means you don't start working on your resume at the last minute. But since you're a blue-chipper, you've got organizational skills. You'll have time to do it right.

NAME AND ADDRESS

You want them to remember your name, so you put it at the top of the page. If possible, use a larger type size than you use on the rest of your resume. If your typewriter or printer doesn't have this capability, there are several other alternatives: rub-on type, lettering templates, or a Kroy lettering machine. Check with your campus book store or copy center if you need help. Include your address and a phone number where you can be reached or a message can be left during working hours. You might want to consider buying or sharing an answering machine. Or you may be able to have messages left with a friend, neighbor, or relative. In some cases you can have messages taken at the departmental headquarters of your academic major.

Example

MARY Q. STUDENT

Campus Box 007	Atlanta, GA 30332	(494) 894-0000

JOB OBJECTIVE

We've already mentioned that the job objective is the most important piece of information on the page. If employers don't see a potential match, they might not look further no matter how outstanding your record. Ideally, the job you're looking for is identical to the one they're trying to fill (see JOB OBJECTIVE COMPONENTS chart.)

Avoid platitudes and vagueness. All graduates want "A challenging position with opportunities for advancement." If this is your stated career objective, you've told an employer nothing.

Give any information that will tell the employer where you would fit best. For instance, identify where you want to work in the company (sales, finance, etc.); you may also want to indicate the key skills you have to offer (administrative, quantitive, etc.). Companies don't hire generic employees. They hire researchers, accountants, and personnel directors.

We also advise against listing plural job objectives unless they are closely related. You wouldn't, for instance, say you were looking for an "entry-level position in sales or research" because it makes you look as if you have no clear career goals. If you are looking at rather different positions with different companies, we strongly recommend a different resume highlighting the appropriate skills and experience for each position. This is where having a generic resume on a computer, whether it's yours or a professional word processor's, is invaluable. When it comes time to apply for a new job, it is easy to rearrange the material.

Use the actual job titles when you know them—catch the employer's attention right away by showing the possibility of a match. However, don't guess if you're not sure. Personnel may be doing the screening, and they might eliminate you if they don't see what they've been told to look for. If you don't know the exact title, use a standard area such as finance, sales, or research.

Everything else on the resume complements the job objective. The education, experience, and skills all show that you can do the job you're trying to get.

Example

OBJECTIVE:	Seek a position as an **Advertising Sales Representative** using my academic background, proven sales skills, and retail experience

Education
List your educational experience in reverse chronological order. If

you went to a prestigious school, highlight that fact by using bold face letters or caps. Be sure to include a high GPA and any honors or awards. List the key courses relevant to the job you are seeking. Omit insignificant schooling such as the summer course you took at the junior college back home. Don't mention your high school unless you went to a truly outstanding one or had an especially distinguished record.

Example

EDUCATION:
St. Anselm's College   GPA: 2.9/4.0
B.A. Communications   6/87

Coursework: Marketing, Advertising, Media Planning, Principles of Persuasion, Managerial Accounting & Control, Consumer Psychology, Communication Ethics & Law, Public Speaking, FORTRAN

Honors and Activities: Dean's List, earned **80%** of college expenses, Young Business Leaders Club

---

SKILLS

As we mentioned in chapter 13, employers want to know what skills you have. You can embed them in your work history, but sometimes it's a good idea to have a separate skills section. There you can highlight the main skills required of the position you're seeking. By doing so you increase your chances of creating a match in the employer's mind.

Use the STAR Technique we discussed in chapter 12: situation, action, results. Positive results create positive reactions. And if you can quantify your results, you're talking in a language employers understand.

Example

Marketing   * Successfully participated in three-month
                           long computer-based marketing game
                           which simulated the soft drink industry

Organizational   * Actively involved in arranging campus
Ability   international festival; responsibilities
                           included: arranging media events,
                           designing pamphlets and coordinating
                           the various committees involved

WORK EXPERIENCE

List in reverse chronological order. Play up your work if it's career-related or requires skills you want to emphasize. Whenever possible, use job descriptions that are results-oriented.

Example

WORK HISTORY:	**MACY'S DEPARTMENT STORE**	
	Sales Representative	9/83-12/86
Retail Sales	Created furniture displays and performed price markdowns which led to **10% increase in departmental sales** for 1985	
Communication Skills	Reinforced and **interpreted company procedures** and policies to new company employees during training periods	

Some students find it helpful to have two separate work sections—career-related, which is prominently displayed, and other work, which goes toward the bottom of the page. If you have paid for your own education or a good portion of it, say so. It indicates that you're hard working and self-sufficient. Even if work is not directly related to your job objective, you often learn skills that are relevant to it. For example, getting customers for a summer lawn care business demonstrates salesmanship.

ADDITIONAL INFORMATION

The blue-chip graduate uses every inch of her resume to her advantage. She lists only information that would be a selling point. Most employers don't really need to know that you enjoy swimming and scuba diving. A marine biologist, however, might find it helpful to include these. An engineer cited her plumbing experience when she applied for a position that required wearing a hard hat. She wanted to show that being a woman didn't mean she was afraid to get her hands dirty. One candidate noted that hunting was one of his hobbies. He was applying for a position in a rural area where hunting was extremely popular. By mentioning his interest in guns, he was able to show that he could be one of the boys even though he'd gone to school in the big city. If you can't find another place to include a selling point, stick it in here. Leave it off it's not relevant.

REFERENCES

Choose them carefully. If you've followed the suggestions in this book, you should have many to choose from. Ask them if they are comfortable writing a favorable recommendation for you. Make sure they have copies of your resume. It will help them to discuss you more knowledgeably when they are contacted by employers. Also, when they see the total package they might be able to come up with other job leads for you. We recommend not listing your references on the resume. It's better to use every precious inch of space to promote yourself.

WORDING AND PHRASING

You control the tone of your resume by the way you write it. There should be no negatives. We remember one student listing a course in which he made a *D*. In fact, that's about all we can remember.

Your resume should be crisp and have punch. Remember, it's your personal ad. Start sentences with verbs or action words, and you'll create the impresssion that you're a "doer," not one who sits and waits. Delete pronouns and anything superfluous.

The whole idea is to boil your marketability down to its essence. Recruiters and interviewers, then, will find it easy to remember you. And why they should hire you. Not every recruiter has been trained in personnel. Frequently corporations send new, inexperienced employees to handle screening interviews at college placement centers. They don't necessarily know how to compare the credentials of the many different candidates. It is to your advantage to make their job easier. A sharp resume is a first step. Make it clear why you're the one their company is looking for.

ACTION WORDS FOR RESUME CONSTRUCTION

A resume will be the first impression an employer has of you. Make it count! Set the tone by using both action and positive words. Starting sentences with verbs can make your message stronger. Be honest, but don't diminish your abilities by using lackluster words.

The following is a list of action words to use in constructing your resume. Refer to it often.

actively	assessed	collaborated	designed	estimated
accelerated	assisted	commended	determined	evaluated
accomplished	attentive	communication	detected	examined
accurately	audited	compiled	developed	executive
achieved	authenticated	completed	devised	exhibited
adapted	budgeted	conducted	directed	expanded
addressed	built	consistently	diverted	expedited
adjusted	calculated	constructed	drafted	experienced
administered	capable	consulted	drew up	explained
adopted	careful	coordinated	earned	expressed
advised	cataloged	contracted	economically	facilitated
analyzed	certified	counseled	edited	familiar (with)
applied	chaired	created	effective	filed
appointed	changed	credited (with)	elected	finalist
appraised	channeled	debated	eliminated	finished
approved	chiefly	decided	enhanced	forecasted
arbitrated	chosen	delegated	enthusiastic	founded
arranged	clarified	delivered	erected	function
assembled	coached	demonstrated	established	generated

graduated	manufactured	primary	reviewed
guided	marketed	principal	satisfactorily
helped	maximum	produced	saved
hired	measurable	proficient	scheduled
honored	mediation	programmed	schematic
illustrated	merchandised	progressed	selected
implemented	merit	projected	served
improved	methodically	promoted	significantly
increased	minimal	proposed	simplified
indexed	moderated	proved	sold
influenced	modified	provided	solved
innovation	most	publicized	solution
inspected	motivated	qualified	specialized
installed	motorized	quoted	spoke
instituted	narrated	recommended	stabilized
instrumental	navigated	recorded	strategy
integrated	negotiated	reduced (losses)	streamlined
interpreted	obtained	reinforced	structured
interviewed	organized	renovated	successfully
judged	originated	reorganized	suggested
knowledgeable	overcame	reported	summarized
launched	participated	represented	supervised
lead	perceptive	researched	supplemented
lectured	performed	resolved	supported
licensed	persuaded	responsible	surveyed
lobbied	pinpointed	responsibilities	systematized
logical	planned	restored	taught
maintained	positive	revamped	trained
major	prepared	revenue	upgraded
managed	presented	revised	wrote

TYPES OF RESUMES
Chronological
This is the most traditional type—which is its advantage. Employers are familiar with it. The disadavantage of the chronological resume is that it plays up your work history even if it's sketchy or unrelated to your job obejctive. If you've followed the blue-chip Master Plan, you should have a solid work history. If your professional experience is weak, consider another type of resume.

Functional
Since work history is played down, you can emphasize the skills necessary to perform the job you're seeking. And since you're not following any prescribed order, you can position the most relevant skills, experience, for example, higher on the page. Its main disadvantage is that employers see fewer of this type, and that might bother some of them. Of course, it might also catch their eye.

Hybrid
We believe there is nothing sacred about resume construction. Your ultimate goal is to create a message that effectively promotes you. We read the resume experts, and we considered the principles of advertising. We did some research of our own—asking recruiters and personnel directors how they appraised resumes. Our guidelines evolved from all these sources. But they're still only guidelines.

Different students may have unique situations that require novel resumes. What about the student who makes a dramatic shift in educational focus? How can you get the most mileage out of a double major or a dual degree program? Nontraditional students also present unique problems. How do you highlight your strengths if you're a middle-aged homemaker returning to the work force? (Returning to the *paid* work force would be more accurate.) Or suppose you're returning to school after a substantial work history. Here are three resumes that break the rules, but we think they come out stronger for doing so.

SHIFT IN EDUCATIONAL FOCUS

DONNA SALERNO

1751 East Lansing Avenue   TACOMA, WA 98401   206/758-8610

OBJECTIVE

Seek a position as an **applications programmer** in the area of database management systems applying my computer skills and management background

EDUCATION

UNIVERSITY OF PUGET SOUND   GPA: 3.37/4.0
  B.S.   Computer Science/Business   6/87

  Coursework: Emphasis on database management systems, including: Business Data Processing, Assembly Language and Computer Architecture, Database Management Systems, Information Storage and Retrieval, and File Processing

QUALIFICATIONS

Programming: Proficient in **FORTRAN, PASCAL, "C," dBASE III, BASIC,** R:BASE 5000, and LOTUS 1-2-3; knowledgeable in COBOL, 8088 and Motorola 6800 assembly language, and UNIX operating system

Hardware: Experienced in use of CDC Cyber, Harris 800, **IBM S/34** and S/36, VAX, IBM PC, and Hewlett-Packard mainframe

Software design: Developed a **relational database system** for a class project that provides a statistical summary of the ongoing programs at a heavily utilized center for the handicapped

Project Develoment: Successfully developed and managed a federally funded project with a **budget of two million dollars** and a **staff of twenty-five**, including all phases of contract administration: i.e., grant acquisition, total budget control, supervising, hiring and firing personnel

WORK HISTORY

CENTER FOR REHABILITATION AND TESTING   7/78-present
  Senior Social Worker   Tacoma, WA
GEORGE H. LANIER MEMORIAL HOSPITAL   3/75-6/78
  Activity/Social Service Consultant   Tacoma, WA
ADULT SERVICES—WASHINGTON DEPARTMENT
OF PENSIONS & SECURITIES   9/65-12/74
  Social Worker II   Seattle, WA

ADDITIONAL EDUCATION

SAN DIEGO STATE UNIVERSITY   M.S.W. Social Work   1965
SAN DIEGO STATE UNIVERSITY   A.B. Social Work   1964

ACTIVITIES:

- Selected as **host family** for 5 foreign exchange students from Denmark, Holland and Sweden
- Member, Association of Rehabilitation Programs in Data Processing
- Member, **Association for Computing Machinery**

REFERENCES FURNISHED UPON REQUEST

FUNCTIONAL RESUME

BENNETT TINDALL

Post Office Box 15933
Atlanta, Georgia 30332
404/892-4400

OBJECTIVE:

Seek position as an **industrial designer** using strong design and project management skills

EDUCATION:

GEORGIA INSTITUTE OF TECHNOLOGY
6/87

B.S.
Industrial
Design

Concentrated in product package, exhibit and graphic design; additional courses included production processes and materials, computer-aided design (CAD), ergonomics, and solid modeler experience

DUKE UNIVERSITY   6/86-9/86

Studies Abroad
Program/France

Studied art history and figure drawing; traveled throughout Europe for two months

QUALIFICATIONS:

Product Design

Concept model of **mobile parapodium** retained by Atlanta's Henrietta Eggleston Hospital for further development

Computer-Aided Design

Proficient in **solid modeler** and design drafting techniques

Project Management

Served as **President** and **Board Member** for campus organization; responsibilities included revising and implementing annual budget, organizing programs and events, and proposing ideas and strategies for annual goals

WORK HISTORY:

Contributed **60%** of college expenses through work and financial aid as follows:

Delivery Manager

FUN COMPANY, INC.   Summers 1985-85
Coordinated, scheduled, and produced employee picnics and conventions; **supervised** staffing groups of 20-60

ACTIVITIES:

President and Board Member, Black Student Fellowship-3 years; **Dean's List**; staff artist for student newspaper

**REFERENCES AND PORTFOLIO AVAILABLE
UPON REQUEST**

CHRONOLOGICAL RESUME

ANDREW FOENSTER

Campus Address: P.O. Box 64902, St. Cloud, MN 56301 612/255-9000
Permanent Address: 17 Faribault Place, Omaha, NB 68178 402/448-6413

OBJECTIVE: Position as **Medical Technologist** in clinical laboratory

EDUCATION:

ST. CLOUD STATE UNIVERSITY   12/87
B.S. Medical Technology

LINCOLN COMMUNITY COLLEGE   8/84
A.S. General Sciences

Significant Coursework:

- Hematology
- Immunology
- Clinical Chemistry
- Histology
- Microbiology
- Microscopy
- Immunohematology
- Cell Biology

WORK EXPERIENCE:

HENNEPIN COUNTY MEDICAL CENTER
Intern Technologist   Minnneapolis, MN
                                            1/86 - present

Performed **microscopic examinations** of blood and bone
marrow. Isolated and identified **microbiological cultures**.
Conducted **renal function tests** including chemical and
microscopic examinations of body fluid analysis. Performed and
correlated **serological testing**.

BHP, INC.   Redland, MN
Operator I / Operator II   10/84 - 11/85

Manufactured **blood references** for Coulter counters and
other specialized medical uses. Mixed chemical solutions,
washed blood, sampled materials, mixed blood solutions to
specified concentrations of various cell types. **Promoted** from
operator I to operator II in three weeks.

GREATER LINCOLN BLOOD PROGRAM
Interviewed prospective donors   Lincoln, NB
                                              Summers 1983/84

ACTIVITIES:

Provided **100%** of college expenses; member, **Medical
Technology Association;** member, St. Cloud State Ski Club

REFERENCES AVAILABLE UPON REQUEST

DOUBLE MAJOR

MYRA SANDERSON

1299 Big Oak Lane   New Orleans, LA 70118   (504) 233-1975

OBJECTIVE: Seek position as a **technical writer** applying my communication skills and scientific background

EDUCATION: **LOYOLA UNIVERSITY**   GPA: 3.0/4.0
B.S. Botany   9/87
B.A. English

Double Major   **Coursework:** Technical Writing; Style and Editing in Technical Writing; Advanced Technical Writing; Computer Documentation; Ecology; Genetics; Taxonomy

Honors and Activities: Dean's List; member, Technical Communicators of America; programs chairman, Alpha Omega Pi Sorority; earned **60%** of college expenses

CAREER-RELATED EXPERIENCE: **LOYOLA UNIVERSITY**
Biology Dept.   9/86-present
Technical Assistant   New Orleans, LA

Technical Editing   Wrote and edited technical **documentation** ranging from explanation of laboratory processes to final reports submitted to government sponsors

GULF COAST RESEARCH LABORATORY   Summer, 1986
Intern   Ocean Springs, MS

Technical Writing   Collaborated on research and development of **extensive report** analyzing effects of erosion on coastal vegetation

SKILLS:
Communication: Coordinated two outdoor campus events for over **1000** participants each, one of which produced the **largest profit to date** for that event

Computer: Proficient in DOS, **BASIC, LOTUS 1-2-3,** WordStar, and Volkswriter. Experienced in use of IBM PC, and CDC Cyber

ADDITIONAL WORK HISTORY   LOYOLA STUDENT ATHLETIC COMPLEX   9/85-6/86
Equipment Attendant
POPEYE'S FRIED CHICKEN
RESTAURANT   1/83-6/85
Cashier

REFERENCES FURNISHED UPON REQUEST

HOMEMAKER

MARIAN SMITHERMAN

1616 Mockingbird Lane
Kendrick, Idaho 83840
(208) 446-6111

OBJECTIVE: Seek position as **Management Trainee in retail sales organization** using my supervisory ability, marketing and administrative skills

EDUCATION

B.S. **University of Idaho** 1/88
Business GPA: 3.3/4.0

Coursework: Management Theory; Marketing; Consumer Behavior; Retailing; Organization Theory; Sales Force Management; Promotional Strategy

EXPERIENCE AND QUALIFICATIONS

Management: Supervised operations for annual fund-raising art exhibit, auction, and formal dinner; hired and trained personnel for event which raised over $10,000

Manage seven **rental properties** for small real-estate agency; supervise custodial operations, lease negotiations and enforcements, and rental collections

Sales & Developed and implemented **advertising**
Marketing: **campaign** and merchandise displays for church thrift shop; **sales increase by 30%** in first month of operation

Administration: **Maintained budget,** including payroll, accounts receivable and payable for church thrift shop

Coordinated feasibility study of community theater renovation; successfully presented proposal to city government resulting in an assistance grant

Design: Designed stage scenery and selected costumes for community theater production; play noted by city newspaper as being "visually exciting"

WORK HISTORY

Dundee & Smitherman Realtors 1975-present
St. Jude's Thrift Shop 1979-1984
Family Management &
Independent Study 1971-1984

REFERENCES FURNISHED UPON REQUEST

RESUMES WHILE IN SCHOOL

Most blue-chippers look for jobs several times while they're in college. This can begin the second quarter of your freshman year if you're a co-op student. Part-time work, summer jobs, and internships also require some sophistication about the process of getting hired. (Chapter 6 explains the importance of work experience.)

Application Form

In most instances you'll have to fill out a standard application or data sheet when applying for a job. We strongly recommend that you supplement it with your own personal resume. Personnel forms are designed to compare all applicants on certain key categories—school, work, etc. It's harder to emphasize your strong points if you don't have top grades or an impressive work history. A personal resume gives you more flexibility. You can highlight whatever you choose. And including a quality personal resume makes you look more professional.

There are a few things that you can do to beef up the form that personnel sends you. Usually there will be a place for "Additional Information." Consider listing skills pertinent to the job in question here. (Once more the STAR Technique helps you to shine.) Try to use every bit of available space to convey pertinent information about you. On the back of some forms there is space for listing coursework and a small "Comments" section. Cite only the most relevant courses and/or those in which you made the best grades. If you write across the page, separating courses with commas, you'll have more room to cover skills and other pertinent information.

Job Objective

Be wary of being too specific when applying for summer jobs. Many employers don't want to hire someone for a narrowly focused area for two or three months. The exception to this rule is when the work is seasonal or consists of a time-limited project. When stating your job objective for part-time, long-term work, follow the same principles you would when applying for permanent, full-time positions.

If you're applying for a co-op position or an internship, identify the area where you want to work. You probably won't start on anything very high up the ladder. Expect some on-the-job training first.

SAMPLE JOB OBJECTIVES

Seeking summer employment in a hospital using my pre-nursing training

Seeking summer employment in surveying using my civil engineering training

Seeking part-time employment in retail sales

Seeking part-time employment (10-20 hours/week) as electronics repairman

Business major desires co-operative placement in marketing or sales

Seek internship with government agency utilizing my two years of undergraduate education in Political Science and History

Other Information

Emphasize any high-school honors and achievements. Do the same for your collegiate record to date. Include data from high school that pertains to skills, work history, and activities.

STUDENT RESUME

CHRIS SHORE

Box 599 Holcomb, University of Arkansas, Fayetteville, AR 72701
501/555-5438

JOB OBJECTIVE: Summer internship with a **daily newspaper,** using
my **journalistic training** and **writing skills**

EDUCATION

- **UNIVERSITY OF ARKANSAS**   Journalism major   GPA: 3.5
  Honors Program   1984-present
- **FAYETTEVILLE HIGH SCHOOL**   graduated June, 1984

CAREER-RELATED EXPERIENCE

UNIVERSITY OF ARKANSAS PRESS   June, 1984-present
- Assistant, Promotion and Marketing
  In charge of **promotion** for *VINEGAR DAYS,* by Max Middlesex

- Intern
  Wrote **jacket copy** and designed **advertising layouts** for
  national authors; collaborated on coordinating autographings;
  ACCOMPLISHMENT: Consistently high appraisals resulted in
  promotion to salaried position

SKILLS

- **EDITING & PUBLISHING:** Currently being trained in
  manuscript and newspaper editing by University of
  Arkansas Press; editor of high-school newspaper;
  ACCOMPLISHMENT: Received **superior rating** from
  Arkansas High-School Press Association for editorial on
  possible teacher strike
- **INTERVIEWING: Feature editor** and **reporter** for high-school
  newspaper; **ACCOMPLISHMENT:** Received **superior rating**
  from Arkansas High-School Press Association for interview
  with city government leader
- **LEADERSHIP:** Participated in "CLOSE-UP" political awareness
  program for a week in Washington, DC; Student Body President,
  Alday Junior High School
- **PRODUCTION:** Experienced in all phases of publication
  production, including copy preparation, design, typesetting, and
  keylining

ADDITIONAL WORK HISTORY

- Grocery Clerk, IGA, Summer, 1985
- Sales Clerk, McGuire's Book Shop, Atlanta, GA, Summer, 1984
- Grocery Clerk, IGA, Summer, 1984

REFERENCES AVAILABLE UPON REQUEST

STUDENT RESUME

NICHOLAS BENNINGS

Campus: 37-G Addison Hall, Bates College, Lewiston, ME
Permanent: 1301 Dalrymple, Hartford, CT 06110, 203/299-4636

JOB OBJECTIVE: Seek internship or summer employment with a **metropolitan museum** using my communication skills and interests in art history and anthropology

EDUCATION:

BATES COLLEGE   GPA: 3.7/4.0
     1986-present

**Anthropology
Major**

- Social Anthropology Course
- Cultural Anthropology Course
- Greek and Roman Art and Architecture Course
- Art of the Middle Ages Course
- Dean's List first semester
- Member, The Arts Society

MERRIMAC HIGH SCHOOL   GPA:3.5/4.0

**Advanced
Curriculum**

- Advanced English, social sciences   1982-1986
- President, Art Club
- National Honor Society member

EXPERIENCE:

**VANDERNESSEN MUSEUM
OF FINE ARTS**   Summer, 1986

Volunteer

- Worked with curator to set up museum exhibits
- Prepared art objects for shipment

FUN WORLD AMUSEMENT PARK   Summer, 1985

**Games
Host**

- Developed strong **communication** and **public-relations skills** through heavy customer contact

References furnished upon request.

BLUE-CHIP COVER LETTERS

Cover letters should be strong enough to stand on their own and promote you even when separated from your other credentials. In other words, no "Dear Mr. Gronk, I'm interested in working for your organization. Enclosed, please find my resume. Sincerely . . ."

Use the cover letter to elaborate on any information that is briefly covered in the resume and is a selling point. Use key phrases taken from your resume. Advertising relies on repeated presentations, and you're advertising yourself. "Where's the beef?" is probably still familiar to you several years after the ad stopped running because you heard it so many times.

Format

The opening paragraph needs to serve as a "hook." It should motivate employers to read further. Mentioning something interesting about the company (not just something found in the Yellow Pages) shows that you believe their company is worth spending time on. Like the resume, the cover letter needs to show how a candidate's skills meet the employer's needs. State specifically how you can help solve the employer's problems. Indicate why you're contacting the employer and how you found out about the job (magazine article, newspaper ad, professional contact, etc.).

You'll probably need to do some research in sources such as the *Business Periodical Index, Reader's Guide, Moody's Index*, and *Dun's Career Guide*. Chapter 16 describes how to research a company in much greater detail. Say specifically why you're interested in the particular organization you're contacting.

Body of Letter

Present your case as a strong candidate. Briefly cite whichever of your academic achievements, skills, accomplishments, and work history is relevant. Give specific examples with details. Repeat some of the key phrases contained in your resume to reinforce your selling points. Tell them "where the beef is." Mention enclosing a resume for their convenience.

February 2, 1987

Museum of Natural Artifacts
    And History
1748 Lincoln Square
New York, NY 10025

Attn: Mr. Carson Donnelly,
        Director of Student Internship Program

Dear Mr. Donnelly:

I am interested in applying for a summer internship offered
through the Museum of Natural Artifacts and History. *American
Historian* magazine recently reported that the MNAH provided
the "most extensive training—outside of a dig—to those students
interested in archaeology and anthropology." Although you have
twenty-five summer internships, it's obvious that you have to be
selective in choosing participants. Here's why I can make a
positive contribution.

First, I have prior experience working in a museum. While in high
school I was a volunteer at the Vandernessen Museum of Fine
Arts. There I helped the curator set up exhibits and prepare art
objects for shipment. One project that I particularly enjoyed
working on included over 250 Indian artifacts and featured a full-
scale replica of a wigwam.

Second, my academic accomplishments include a GPA of 3.7 after
one semester as an anthropology major at Bates College and
membership in the National Honor Society.

Finally, I have strong communication and leadership skills. I have
proven experience in leading groups, being a team member, and
working with the public, all assets that are helpful in a museum
environment.

I have enclosed a resume for your convenience. I am eager to
discuss internship opportunities and will contact you in three
weeks to arrange an interview.

Sincerely,

Nicholas Bennings

Nicholas Bennings
37-G Addison Hall
Bates College
Lewiston, ME 04240

Closing Paragraph

Ask for action. Be confident and assertive about doing so. You wouldn't apply for the job if you didn't think you were the right one to do it. State that you will contact them in ten days to two weeks. *And do it.*

Note how Nicholas Bennings's cover letter complements his resume. Either letter or resume can stand alone, but together they build an even stronger case for the candidate.

Rather than conclude with our usual chapter summary, we leave you with a Resume Checklist. Use it every time you make out your resume.

RESUME CHECKLIST

You want your resume to be memorable to the employer—but for all the right reasons. An omission or mistake should not be noted as your resume's most outstanding feature. Use this chart to check for any oversights. Have it double-checked by a friend just to ensure you haven't missed anything.

DID YOU:	YES	NO
1. Prominently display your name?		
2. Put in a complete address and zip code?		
3. List a daytime telephone number and area code?		
4. Specify your job objective?		
5. Position your strongest information first?		
6. Describe your education?		
7. Complete a work experience section?		
8. Detail your relevant skills?		
9. Include information on affiliations?		
10. Use both positive and action words?		
11. Check for accuracy of information— names, dates,etc.?		
12. Verify technical terms and descriptions?		
13. Correct any poor grammar?		
14. Shorten or tighten sentences?		
15. Eliminate repetitiveness?		
16. Leave out anything important?		

15
How To Be
A Silver-Tongued Devil:
Interviewing

It's been four months since Sam Dresden's disastrous interview with HealthCo. Today, he's scheduled to talk with a representative from Mega, Inc. Let's see if he's learned from his mistakes.

He gets up a half-hour earlier than usual and takes an invigorating shower. He pulls his freshly pressed interviewing suit from the closet and gets dressed. After a light breakfast he makes the twenty-minute drive down to Mega. He checks his watch. Ten till. Good. He can check his appearance in the restroom mirror and still have time to go over his notes. Aside from a little nervous energy, he's feeling confident. He should be. This time he's ready.

Sam was depressed after his fiasco with HealthCo, but he didn't stay down. He knew he had to do something different, or he'd never get a good job. So he found out all he could about getting hired.

He attended a job-search workshop that Placement offered. He talked to friends, including Sally Kowalski, who had landed good positions. He read a book on interviewing. He even talked to a couple of businessmen his father knew so he could get a feel for the employer's perspective.

Gradually things fell into place. Sam finally realized that interviewing could be simplified into one proposition:

Convince the employer that you match his needs.

He knew this wasn't always easy, but it helped to focus on just one objective. Especially when it was the same objective behind his resume, his cover letter, all his communication with employers. His confidence grew, and he started feeling hopeful again.

INTERVIEWING GAME PLAN

Before the Interview

1. Conduct a thorough self-assessment (goals & skills).
2. Develop a good resume.
3. Research the company and industry.
4. Anticipate key questions and develop effective answers.
5. Have your interview wardrobe ready.

During the Interview

1. Be confident and relaxed.
2. Follow the interviewer's cues.
3. Show enthusiasm.
4. Emphasize your selling points.
5. Sell yourself as a match.
6. Ask intelligent questions.

After the Interview

1. Write notes about the interview.
2. Send a thank-you letter.

GETTING READY

A good coach never brings his team out on the field without first preparing the players for the game. They need to know who they're up against, what to expect, and how to score points. Otherwise, they might as well stay in the locker room.

It's the same with interviewing. The more you know about the company, the questions they'll ask, and how to sell yourself, the better your chances for getting an offer. There are four preparation steps.

1. Develop A Marketable Resume

By now you should have a winning resume. If you haven't, go back to Chapter 14 and pull one together. Make sure that your references have copies of your resume. It could be embarrassing for both of you if they have to "wing it" when employers call them. Besides, they might not remember all your shining qualities without a little prompting.

Keep your resume and calendar by the telephone. If an unexpected call from an employer turns into a telephone interview, you'll be at your best in discussing your qualifications — even if you're dripping wet. Also, you'll impress them with your time-management skills if you don't have to fumble at setting a time.

2. Anticipate Key Questions.

Randall Powell in *Career Planning Today* says that interviewers want the answers to four questions:
1. What are your qualifications?
2. Do your qualifications match our needs?
3. Why are you interested in our company?
4. Are you the best person for the job?

To get answers to these questions, they'll probe your background with other additional questions. Some may seem unrelated or vague. Some might make you sweat. But unless the interviewer is a rookie or a real sadist, her questions have a purpose. She's trying to find out if you're the right person for the job.

The questions can be open-ended: "Tell me about yourself." They can be very specific: "Explain why your grades are low." We've included a list of the most commonly asked questions.

QUESTIONS INTERVIEWERS ASK

Tell me about yourself.

Why do you feel qualified for this position?

What would you consider an ideal job?

What do you know about our company?

What are your short-term goals? Your long-term goals?

What are your strengths? Your weaknesses?

What have been your most satisfying and disappointing experiences?

Why did you major in _____?

Which courses did you like best?

Explain why your grades are low.

How did you finance your education?

Do you plan to continue your education?

What did you learn from your work experience? From school?

What managerial or leadership positions have you held?

Why did you leave your job(s)?

How long do you plan on being with us if we hire you?

Tell me about your extracurricular activities.

What was the last book you read?

Where would you like to work? (geographic area)

Are there any places you wouldn't want to work?

Are you willing to relocate?

How do you feel about putting in overtime?

Have answers ready for these questions. And remember, when Ms. Manager says, "Tell me about yourself," she doesn't really want to know who you had a crush on in the sixth grade or why you think hang gliding is totally awesome. She wants to know about your achievements, your career goals, and why you chose your major. The bottom line is always: Can you meet the needs of our company?

The STAR Technique (Situation-Action-Results) is a powerful way for you to show her that you can. See Chapter 12 if you need a quick refresher. Armed with a list of your skills in academic, extra-curricular, and work situations you can face even the toughest questions. The STAR Technique is especially helpful in fielding open-ended questions (Tell me about your extracurricular activities) and handling stress questions (Why should I hire you?). You can also use it to keep a digressing interviewer on target.

Outline responses to difficult or complicated questions. When discussing your weaknesses make sure your response doesn't conclude with a statement that leaves a negative impression. Counter the negative by adding something positive:

My GPA is lower than I would like because I had to work twenty hours a week to put myself through school. I was still able to graduate in four years, and I feel I learned a lot on the job.

Or:

I wasn't sure of my major when I started school, and my grades reflected that. Once I settled on journalism, my GPA started to pick up.

Spend extra time preparing for "loaded" questions. You should never lie, but an employment interview is not the time to purge your soul of any doubts or ambivalence you might be feeling. A good reply to "How long do you plan on being with us if we hire you?" might be "I'm looking at this job as a career opportunity, not as a short-term position." You've shown your commitment to the company and indicated you view it as more than a stepping stone—both things the interviewer wants to hear.

Questions You'll Want To Ask

Your questions are important too. Remember, you're also evaluating them. Can they meet your needs? Besides, what you ask says something about you—your enthusiasm, your maturity, your understanding of the problems facing your field. Never ask obvious questions, ones that could be answered by reading the company brochure. Also, steer away from questions about salary, vacation, and company benefits during an initial contact—that is, unless the interviewer brings them up.

Speaking of initial contact, bear in mind that screening interviews serve a different purpose than the round of interviews conducted on a plant trip. Your interview at the Placement Office will probably last about thirty minutes. The person who conducts it probably does not have the power to hire you. Your purpose is to stay in the running by not getting screened out. That is why you don't want to be pushy about salary and benefits. Those kinds of questions are more appropriately raised at the final stages of the interviews conducted on the actual work site.

Be sure to ask specific questions about the job as it relates to your background. For instance, ask about the hardware and software used if you're a computer programmer. Ask about laboratory equipment if you're a medical technician. A coach might want to know about the practice facilities and the equipment budget.

SUGGESTED QUESTIONS TO ASK

What can I expect the first month on the job? The first three months? The first six months?

Have you hired many graduates with a background similar to mine?

Is the job currently filled?

Why is the job open now?

What is a typical career path for this position?

What is your relocation policy?

How much travel is involved?

How can I become immediately productive in this job?

What opportunities are there for in-service training and professional development?

How would you characterize the managerial philosophy of the firm?

What have those who have previously filled this position liked best about it? Least?

3. Research the company thoroughly.

You can't make a strong case for being hired if you don't know anything about them. How does an employer know you'll be a help if you can't show you understand their needs? And just as important, how do you know they're the right company for you? After all, you'll be spending an average of two thousand hours a year for these people. That's a heavy commitment to rush into blindly, so find out what you can about a prospective employer.

We have focused heavily on the business world because the majority of graduates end up working there. We talk a lot about researching corporations. This is because there is greater access to information about the corporate world. Yet many of you will work for schools, hospitals, governmental agencies, small businesses and so on. But the same principles apply in each case. The more you know about a prospective employer, the better off you are.

Categories To Consider When Researching A Company

1. *What the company does:* Sell a product or a service? How diversified is its line? A multinational corporation may have hundreds. A small private school, just one.
2. *The stability of the organization:* What is the outlook of the industry and the particular company? How big were sales last year? Is the company growing? Who are the competitors? What about the company's reputation? Are there plans for new products or divisions? The idea is to avoid climbing aboard a sinking ship. Or better yet, to get in just before the company takes off.
3. *How the company operates:* What is its organizational structure? Are there many levels of employees or just a few? Is it publicly owned, a Mom and Pop store, or a governmental agency? How large? Where located? More than one location? What is management like? How old? How qualified? How did they get there? Are there training programs for employees? What is the typical path for someone with your career objective? How are the employees treated? What about salaries? Benefits? Is there a recognizable corporate philosophy?

Sources Of Information About A Company

As mentioned earlier, it is easier to research a corporation than the corner drugstore. Perhaps it would be more accurate to say that you have to rely on different sources to investigate a small organization. Generally speaking, you will have to rely on word of mouth. If you've followed the Master Plan, you will already know people in your field. You can develop other sources of information through networking. Touch as many bases as you can, and see what you can find out.

Here are some other tips when researching a smaller organization:

Check with professional associations. Is the prospective employer a member? In good standing? Chambers of Commerce, Better Business Bureaus, and Speakers' Bureaus can all provide a few basic facts. In a very small community, the office of the mayor or city manager may serve as a primary source of information. Local newspapers and periodicals are another important source. If you have the gumption to do it, visit a local bar, diner, or restaurant that serves employees or clientele. Strike up a conversation, and see what you can find out.

A nurse applying for a position at a hospital would want to take a look at the hospital's brochure, find out about the demographics of the clientele, and get information on employment practices from Nurses' Associations. Finally, our blue-chip nurse would likely visit with other nurses in the hospital cafeteria or snack bar and pump them for information.

If you're unable to find much information about the particular company you're considering, be sure to research current trends in your field. Having such up-to-date knowledge will help you to ask the key questions to see how an organization measures up. You'll also come across much more impressively during the interview.

If you are researching a large corporation, ask for assistance at the library. Research librarians can provide you with a wealth of material on products, services, and key personnel. Some basic sources to investigate include:

Annual Reports: Every public business is required to publish an annual report. You can get a copy from the firm's public relations department or often from placement offices, career-planning centers, stock brokerage firms, public libraries, etc. It typically contains:

Statement from president
Current activities and future plans
Summary of sales and profits
Independently audited financial statements
Comparison of this year's earnings to last.

Employment Brochures: Organizations which employ several hundred people usually publish employment (recruiting) brochures. These are available through campus placement offices and college libraries. Or you can directly contact the company's college relations or personnel department. These brochures are a good source of information on the corporate environment. Pictures and quotes give you clues about the company's management style.

Investment Reports: Many investment firms make an analysis of public business firms whose stock is available for purchase. These reports may include such information as sales volume, earnings, and current market demand for products. Sources for stock market reports include *Value Line Investment Surveys, Standard and Poor's Stock Reports,* and *Moody's.* You could also contact a brokerage house as a potential client and get information.

Product Information: To learn about the range of products that a particular company manufactures, consult the *Thomas Register,* an eighteen-volume annual publication. Volumes 1-10 are like the yellow pages: under each product category, all manufacturers are listed alphabetically and geographically. Volumes 11-12 name all products made by each company. Volumes 13-18 contain sample pages from company catalogs. You can also get product information from trade magazine ads or from product brochures put out by the company.

Business Periodicals: These are good sources of information about corporate environment and current happenings. Features on top executives give you a feel for the management philosophy of a company. To find magazine articles look under the *Business Periodical Index* and *Reader's Guide to Periodical Literature.* Other sources to consider would include: *Fortune, Forbes, Barron's, Financial World, Business Week,* etc.

4. Have interviewing clothes ready. First impressions may be super-ficial, but they matter. Don't get left at the starting gate because your suit is wrinkled. Have at least one conservative suit that flatters you and makes you feel comfortable. If you need to, ask a more sartorially sophisticated friend to help you pick one out. Or check out John T. Malloy's *Dress For Success* or Susan Bixler's *Professional Image*.

Dress the way successful people in the field you're entering dress. Neat, clean, and currently stylish is what you should aim for. Now is not the time to borrow Dad's leisure suit or Mom's pillbox hat. You may also want to designate a couple of shirts or blouses as off-limits except for interviews. The same with a freshly shined pair of dress shoes and your favorite tie. And after each interview, look over your outfit and put it away for the next time. You don't want any surprise grease spots waiting for you.

DURING THE INTERVIEW

1. Be confident and relaxed. (Step 1 for the actual interview, step 5 for the entire interview process.)

All employers want someone who is self-assured and able to per-form under pressure. Try to look at each interview as an opportunity to do just that. And why shouldn't you be confident? You've worked hard to develop all your blue-chip skills. And you've done your home-work in preparation for the interview itself. Being prepared—it's one of the best ways to feel on top of a situation.

Arrive a few minutes early. You'll have time to check your appear-ance, review your resume, and collect your thoughts. Take note of the surroundings. They can be very revealing—especially if you had a hard time getting information about the organization. Look for com-pany literature in the lobby. Talk with the receptionist. Observe the decor. Is it warm and inviting or cold and formal? All these things are clues to what this outfit is like.

If you're feeling more than the usual nervous energy, you can calm down by using one of the stress management techniques described in Chapter 9.

When you first meet Mr. Manager make eye contact and shake his hand when he offers it. Some male interviewers are unsure of protocol and may not extend a hand to a female candidate. We suggest that she offer him her hand as an ice-breaker.

2. Follow the interviewer's cues.

Wait until the interviewer indicates for you to take a seat. If she obviously stalls about asking—a technique sometimes used in stress interviews—announce to her that you'll sit and wait until she's ready to begin.

If you have the opportunity, take a look around the office before the interview starts in earnest. If the room has family pictures and other homey touches, you're probably dealing with a people person. An impersonal atmosphere tips you off that ideas are this interviewer's preference.

Each interviewer will have his or her own style. But basically there are three methods of interviewing:

Directed;

Non-directed; and

Stress.

Directed: When you deal with someone from personnel, chances are he'll ask specific questions based on an outline. There will probably be a set time limit, which doesn't allow for much wasted talk. These are directed interviews, and they're primarily used by trained interviewers for screening candidates.

Non-directed: The atmosphere is less formal. The questions are broader and more likely open-ended. The candidate is encouraged to talk freely. Inexperienced interviewers are more likely to be non-directed.

Stress: The interviewer uses techniques intended to increase tension—long lapses of silence, penetrating stares, and confrontational questions. The idea is to see how you handle the pressure. You obviously make points by staying calm and collected, but how do you manage this?

First, look at a tough interview as a challenge and an opportunity. You're better prepared than most candidates, so handling an unfriendly interview effectively will only make you look stronger than the others. Second, rehearse with friends, especially if you anticipate a stress interview. Make a game of it. See how impossible you can be with each other. The real interview will seem like a piece of cake in comparison. Third, read up on interviewing. We've included several books in Appendix VI.

3. Show enthusiasm.

It's very discouraging to talk with an employer who seems bored out of his skull by your very presence. Well, interviewers can get discouraged too. They want you to be excited about their company. In fact, your chances of getting an offer are minimal if you don't look like you really want to work for them.

So give a firm handshake, maintain eye contact, lean forward, speak up. Listen closely to the interviewer. Reflect key points in your own words. Ask questions if you need clarification. If an interviewer is convinced that you really hear him, you've won half the battle already.

You've researched the company. Demonstrate this knowledge to the interviewer by asking intelligent questions: "I understand your agency is developing a program to combat adult illiteracy. Can you tell me about some of your plans?"

4. Emphasize your selling points.

One student recently came to Sioux for help after getting a flush letter. He reported that half his interview was wasted on small talk. The recruiter was about the same age as the candidate and shared a similar background. They seemed to hit it off because of their similarities. Unfortunately, this led to little more than a rap session. The interviewer probably concluded that the candidate was a nice guy but didn't have much to offer.

Go into each interview with a mental list of your selling points—the skills and experiences that qualify you for this particular job. *Make sure you discuss each one before the end of the interview.* This is the single most important step in the entire interview. If you run into an inexperienced or unfocused interviewer, be tactfully assertive and take the lead yourself. Here are some suggestions:

That's interesting. Maybe we can talk about that more after the interview.

What you're saying reminds me of _____. Let me tell you what I did.

I've had a similar experience which really tested my _____ skills. Let me tell you about it.

This is where your familiarity with the STAR Technique (Chapter 12) comes in handy. Use it well, and you can concisely tick off your selling points with real impact.

5. Sell yourself as a match.

Not only must you emphasize your selling points, but you must also establish a bridge between your skills and the company's needs. This means that you will highlight some of your qualifications more than others. Specifically, you should dwell on those of your selling points that are most crucial to the performance of the job you are applying for.

Obviously, use your own judgment here. If you're interviewing with a large corporation and hope to move up the corporate ladder, you will want to convince the interviewer that you possess management potential even if your first position has no managerial responsibilities.

6. Ask intelligent questions.

You took the trouble to prepare them. Don't pass up the chance to use them. With practice your confidence will grow, and you'll be able to pose thoughtful questions that occur to you during the course of the interview.

AFTER THE INTERVIEW

1. Make notes about the interview as soon as possible.

Write it down while it's still fresh. Otherwise you might forget something important, or get different companies mixed up. Key bits of data are:

1. *Recruiter's name and title* (double-check the spelling);
2. *What you do next*—submit additional information? contact them by a certain date?;
3. *What they do next*—are there other stages to this company's selection process? additional interviews? when will you hear from them?;
4. *Impressions of the interview*—good and bad points.

This helps you prepare for the next interview.

2. Write a thank-you note.

This is more than being polite—it can close the deal. Use this letter to reiterate briefly why you match their needs. Did you forget to emphasize one of your strengths? Have you thought of any new reasons why you're the best qualified candidate for the position? Be sure to highlight that sort of information.

One co-op student used his thank-you letter to ask to be reconsidered. Another wrote:

I was so interested in the new project you mentioned that I had to find out more about it. I discovered that the laboratory equipment being used is similar to what I have been trained to use.

The thank-you note can be just as powerful in the interviewing process as the cover letter. A strong one can reinforce the idea that you fit the employer's needs. A ho-hum one shows only that your mother raised you right.

SUMMARY

1. Your objective during the interview is to demonstrate that you match the employer's needs.
2. Prepare for the interview by:
   a. developing a good resume;
   b. anticipating key questions;
   c. researching the company thoroughly;
   d. having your interview wardrobe ready.
3. You interview well by:
   a. being confident and relaxed;
   b. following the cues of the interviewer;
   c. showing enthusiasm;
   d. emphasizing your selling points;
   e. selling yourself as a match;
   f. asking intelligent questions.
4. Follow up the interview by:
   a. making notes as soon as possible;
   b. sending a thank-you note.

16
The Blue-Chip Payoff: Choosing The Best Offer

If you've followed the Master Plan, you will probably face a rather pleasant problem as you near graduation. Which of several job offers should you accept? Making this choice should not be too difficult because you will rely on the same principles that have governed your behavior throughout your journey toward success. Choosing a particular job is but an extension of all your other career planning. It requires self-assessment—knowing yourself—and also knowledge of the job world. You must know what your values are and what goals are compatible with those values.

Values are either intrinsic or extrinsic. You can like an activity for its own sake or because it gets you something else that you want. Intrinsic work-related values include service and leadership, as well as finding the tasks that make up a job interesting for their own sake.

Goals are the objectives you set that will enable you to express your values. If someone likes the life sciences and helping others, but also requires a high level of income and prestige, being a physician is a compatible career goal. If income and prestige are less important, then nursing or physical therapy could also be considered.

You've also got to weigh the relative merits of short-term gains versus long-term ones. You might have to choose between a good job with little future and a less attractive job that could pay off in the long run. Choices here can be tricky. If you're too future oriented, you run the risk of never getting job satisfaction in the present. But if you immediately jump at mega bucks, you might be mortgaging your future.

Happily, blue-chippers are usually in a position to find satisfying work that also advances them toward longer range goals. Developing a career is a never-ending process. While there are plateaus that bring a sense of satisfaction, it is a myth to think that there will be a point in time when you've "made it" and can rest on your laurels.

One of the reasons blue-chippers are attractive to employers is that they have experience. They've been active—co-oping and interning, working summers, joining clubs, leading groups, coordinating projects. These same experiences will now help you to make concrete career decisions. You should have a clearer grasp of what your values are because you have tried to implement them in so many different ways. You will likely know more than the average student about the kinds of jobs that match your values, the sort of position that would best fit your needs and abilities, and the organization that you would be happiest working for.

As a blue-chipper you've extended yourself, tested your limits, tried on roles for size. You've immersed yourself in life rather than shrinking from it or simply dreaming about it. And your experiences have increased your self-knowledge. The process of self-discovery never ends for blue-chippers because they're always finding out new things about themselves and the world and also because they don't stop changing and growing. There are always new developments to discover!

THE LOGISTICS OF CHOOSING

Some experts recommend quantifying the various rewards different jobs might offer. We frankly doubt that most jobs can be so simply reduced to numbers. While it's easy to compare different starting salaries, how do you weight money against security? Or the opportunity for creative expression? It's all quite subjective and goes back to how well you know yourself.

While we don't think you can reduce employment decisions to a simple numerical equation, we do advocate getting your thoughts down on paper. There are two kinds of payoffs to any job, satisfactions and rewards; both involve intrinsic and extrinsic factors. Satisfactions include your interest in the work, independence, the opportunity for creative expression. Rewards are easier to measure and include income, vacation, retirement plan. These payoffs can be immediate or long term, so the time frame should also be a consideration. For example, a stressful position with modest pay might still be a good first job if the training, experience, and contacts will accelerate your advancement toward positions that are more rewarding and satisfying.

JOB OFFER WORKSHEET

Satisfactions (Intrinsic Payoffs)

We have listed four satisfactions typically associated with work and have provided space for you to list four more. Place up to three pluses (v) or minuses (w) by each satisfaction according to how well you estimate the job you're being offered will provide that satisfaction for you. Underline those satisfactions that are most important to you, then circle any that are absolute requirements.

1. Work interests you   5._____

2. Leadership opportunities   6._____

3. In-service-training   7._____

4. Humanitarian work   8._____

Rewards (Extrinsic Payoffs)

1. Salary   5._____

2. Benefits package   6._____

3. Advancement opportunities   7._____

4. Location   8._____

Effect On Career Goals

Positive long-range effects are:

Negative long-range effects are:

Other Considerations

First positions in the business world often include travel. Management tends to assume that as a new graduate you will have fewer family responsibilities and so travel will be less of a hardship. Be clear on your own preference and requirements, and don't confuse the two. While resistance to living out of a suitcase is understandable, your refusal to do any traveling will probably be regarded by employers as inflexibility and/or timidity.

In general, most first jobs mean starting at the bottom. Expect your share of scut work, unpleasant assignments, difficult clients. A common complaint of management is that today's graduates want it all without first paying their dues. So be realistic; it's not likely that you're going to start out with a limo and a Lear jet at your disposal.

As in all your professional dealings, do your homework first. Before you get down to negotiating over salary, you should know what the average starting pay is in your field. As a blue-chipper, you should also know what the top salaries are for new employees. Check with placement, the career development center, or with a reference librarian at the main library. Probably most important, use your network of contacts. It is especially helpful to exchange salary and benefits information with others in your field—both last year's graduates and those who are interviewing at the same time you are. This is the only way you can get a clear idea of what the market will bear. And remember, as a blue-chipper you have more bargaining power than most new candidates. It is just possible that you can squeeze some extra dollars out of an employer.

Be sure to get some idea of the schedule and rates of raises that prevail with a prospective employer. Some organizations like to start people off at a modest rate of pay. As new employees prove themselves, they are quickly and handsomely rewarded. A hefty first paycheck might not be such a bargain if you're stuck at that level for a long time and future raises promise to be miniscule.

One of your most important considerations in any first job should be opportunities for training. Developing new skills and acquiring new information are so valuable because they are direct investments in yourself and your future. Your salary and benefits can always be taken away from you. Your knowledge and ability can't. And they are always marketable.

The location of your first job is usually important. But what is also important is your employer's policy for relocation. Frequent moves, particularly with little warning, have a big effect on your quality of life. Also the quality of your marriage if you have married. And if your spouse is also struggling to develop a career, the plot can thicken very fast (and may even curdle). So, try to find out how much mobility is expected of you. It's also important to know where the various branch offices and plants are and where the home office is if that's your ultimate destination.

You should know who your immediate supervisor will be and also who else will be in a position to notice your performance. If you turn lead into gold and nobody knows it, your career is not exactly going to rocket skyward.

Blue-Chip Choices

Remember Sally Kowalski and Sam Dresden from Chapter 2? They've done their resumes, had their interviews, and finally gotten offers. What were their decisions?

First, let's look at their offers. Sally had a number of them because she was an outstanding candidate. She chose to go with HealthCo. Here's why. Of her five offers, their salary was next to the bottom. She was also going to have to move to Chicago, which did not appeal to her. The rest of HealthCo's rewards and satisfactions, however, more than made up for these drawbacks.

The money was adequate for her needs, and she knew HealthCo had a policy of giving big raises early on to new employees who proved they had the right stuff. She was confident that she would earn that kind of raise. She would also have enough vacation time to visit family and friends. And Chicago's airport had direct flights to just about anywhere she would want to go. Moreover, HealthCo had offices and facilities all over the country and a policy of allowing employees considerable latitude in picking a place to settle after five years.

Most important to Sally, the actual job she accepted was exactly what she was looking for. It would enable her to work with people and still use her analytical ability. Her colleagues would be energetic and competent. And HealthCo hired the best consultants in the country to provide in-service training for their employees. She had the feeling that her very first job after graduation was going to be a very good career move.

Sam got two offers. One was in sales on a straight commission basis. He was told that aggressive salesmen made great incomes with Flim-Flam, Inc. This appealed to him, but after investigating them, he found out that their sales force had a very high turnover rate. He turned them down, and went with Mega, Inc. instead.

He had interviewed with Mega several months earlier and had impressed the recruiter in spite of his spotty college record. Although he wasn't given a job offer at the time, Sam felt that his improved resume and interviewing skills had still paid off. The recruiter called him personally to say he regretted being unable to offer a job. They had a long conversation, and Sam was invited to stay in touch.

He gradually realized that he wasn't able to compete with blue-chip graduates such as Sally Kowalski. She had paid her dues, but he still had a ways to go. Rather than whine about his predicament, he arranged another appointment with the same interviewer at Mega.

He again discussed his strengths, but this time he also outlined the kinds of job experience he needed to be a valuable employee. The upshot was that he was able to sell Mega on the idea of hiring him as a paid graduate intern. He would finally get the experience he so sorely lacked, and they would have an energetic employee for nine months. If things went well, he could start as a sales trainee at that time. Finances would be tight at first, but Sam was used to that. And the important thing was that he finally felt he was making some progress.

You might wonder why we include Sam in this discussion of blue-chip choices. The answer is because it's never too late to become a blue-chipper. Once he identified his abilities and clarified his goals, Sam was able to develop a realistic strategy that would get results.

And so we have come full circle. We started with today's college students' dreams of career success. We have given you a plan for turning those dreams into reality. Now it's up to you.

17
The Blue-Chip Concept

Blue-chip isn't a fat wallet or a fancy job title. It's an attitude that permeates a person's thoughts and daily life. Blue-chip character and action may result in money and position, but the very essence of being blue-chip boils down to being goal-directed.

Everybody has dreams, but rarely do they make them come true. Blue-chippers have goals and a plan for reaching them. It is common to have aspirations, but wishing, by itself, brings nothing. Blue-chippers have objectives that they accomplish day by day, week by week, year by year.

Developing clear, realistic goals requires both self-understanding and knowledge of the world. Blue-chippers are constantly learning about both by immersing themselves in constructive activity. Life for them is an adventure in which they continually check their values and abilities, goals and plans against experience. They try different courses, jobs, tasks, and roles on for size. They learn from experts, advisors, teachers, books, mentors, and counselors. Gradually they discover what they want and how to get it.

They work hard, and they work smart to get where they're going. It takes both. Effort without direction or focus brings only chaos and turmoil. Goals and talent count for nothing without drive. So blue-chippers strive toward their goals, but they strive wisely. They learn from their experience, and they learn from the experts. They develop their talents. They acquire new skills. They get organized. They're efficient.

Blue-chippers are also persistent. They have to be because no matter how hard and smart they work, there are always obstacles to overcome and rivers to cross. They get back up after they've been knocked down. They keep on keeping on. Failure is never final. It's just another word for feedback. Blue-chippers learn from their setbacks and adjust their goals and plans accordingly.

We obviously think the blue-chip mindset is important, or we wouldn't have written a book about it. But we also offer two words of caution. Being goal-directed is no better than the target you're aiming for. Napoleon was a great general—he almost conquered the world. But his egomania caused untold death and destruction. Hitler ran a successful death camp. It's not just success that makes life meaningful. It's succeeding at something worthwhile.

Another pitfall to goal-directedness is that you will almost certainly be tempted to compromise higher principles in order to reach your goals. In the nineteenth century, American robber barrons made fortunes, and the common good be damned. Today, financier Ivan Boesky has made millions on Wall Street, but he apparently used illegal insider information to do it.

We don't want students who cheat on their anatomy exams to be our next generation of medical doctors. Don't risk your future or your integrity by compromising your principles.

So, set some goals you can be proud of. Develop a plan for reaching them. Work hard, and use your resources. Why not start right now?

APPENDIX I

MASTER PLAN

FRESHMAN YEAR

A company's success doesn't start with it's first million. It starts years earlier with planning. And you must plan too if you hope to become a blue-chip graduate. You begin your Freshman year by developing organizational skills and learning how to study effectively. You take your first steps toward clarifying career goals and assessing your skills. You find out about career-related work and develop a stress management plan.

Develop Organizational Skills

- Set daily, weekly and quarterly goals.
- Maintain a daily and weekly schedule.
- Outline a quarterly class schedule.
- Keep a calendar with important dates marked.
- Develop a file system for school work and personal information.

Learn and Practice Study Skills

- Learn how to use the library.
- Review material immediately after class.
- Avoid cramming or marathon study sessions.
- Learn effective reading, writing and notetaking techniques.

Seek Career Counseling

- Do a thorough self-assessment.
- Determine compatibility of majors to your interests and abilities.
- Explore various career fields.
- Investigate coursework required for different majors.
- Find out programs and resources available to you.

Assess Functional Skills

- Determine what skills you have now that are marketable.
- Find ways to increase their marketability.
- Explore skills needed for different career interests.

Investigate Cooperative Plans, Internships, or Career-Related Employment

- Attend programs sponsored by campus cooperative office.
- Discuss co-op experience with other students.
- Check library for company information on co-op plans and/or internships.
- Make contacts with alumni in career-related fields who might hire students for summer or part-time work.
- Ask professors about possible leads for internships and companies who hire students.

Stress Management Skills

- Develop an exercise program.
- Maintain a healthy diet and good sleeping habits.
- Use tension reduction methods
- Keep a positive attitude.
- Talk to a counselor.

SOPHOMORE YEAR

You use your organizational, study, and stress management skills throughout your collegiate career. You declare a major and begin to consider electives. You join a professional organization and contribute to it. You develop job search skills and secure career related employment.

Declare Major

- Plan a schedule for taking required course work.
- Get to know your advisor.
- Look for electives that are compitible with your interests and complement your major.

Join Professional Association

- Join student chapter affilated with your major.
- Attend local meetings regularly.
- Be as active as your schedule will allow.
- Develop contacts by attending national meetings, conferences and/or seminars whenever convenient.

Secure Career-Related Employment

- Begin co-op or part-time career related job.
- Assess which skills are most required by entry-level graduates in that company.
- Seek work assignments that will help develop skills in areas you are lacking.
- Develop contacts for mentoring and future employment.

Seek Leadership Positions

- Develop good communication skills by public speaking and/or group management.
- Develop ability to manage projects.

Develop Job Search Skills

- Reevaluate your marketable skills.
- Learn the STAR Technique.
- Write a strong resume that stresses your skills.
- Attend job search workshops when available.
- Learn basics of interviewing for information.

JUNIOR YEAR

You assume more active and responsible positions in your extra-curricular activities. You cultivate contacts on and off campus. You learn about specialized areas in your chosen field and corporations that hire the specialists. You find out about graduate and professional schools.

Evaluate Chosen Field

- Reassess how marketable your field is by doing research into who's hiring.
- Talk to your professors and employers.
- Visit your library, counseling center and placement office.
- Check out job qualifications necessary in your field.
- Find out academic requirements.
- Investigate specialized areas of your chosen field.
- Research academic requirements, including graduate school, required for specialization.

Research Functional Employment Areas

- Research standard company divisions, such as: research and development, administration, personnel and finance, etc.
- Assess the compatibility of your skills and interests with the different functional employment areas.
- Interview for information.

Research Graduate or Professional Schools of Your Choice

- Determine the benefits of an advanced degree in your field.
- Conduct thorough search into noteworthy programs in your field by talking to professors and employers and doing library research.
- Research other factors involved: cost, location, faculty, research being done, financial aid, prerequisites, and admission policies.
- Apply for graduate or professional school entrance exams.
- Choose several schools where you would like your entrance exam scores forwarded.

Seek Leadership Positions

- Continue to develop strong communcations and managerial skills.
- Develop contacts for mentoring and possible job leads.

SENIOR YEAR

You're almost there! Apply for graduate programs and take entrance exams if you plan to get an advanced degree. Gear up for the job search by writing your resume and preparing for interviews.

Take Graduate or Professional School Entrance Exams

- Prepare for exams thoroughly.
- Check campus resources for available preparatory programs.
- Check bookstores and library for preparatory books.
- Arrive at test site early and well rested. Be prepared for 3-4 hour test session.

Arrange for Interviews Through Campus Placement Office

- Attend programs explaining procedures of placement office.
- Follow all procedures carefully.
- Maintain contact with Placement Office staff.

Write a Winning Resume

- Develop a clear job objective.
- Detail skills or experience using STAR Technique.
- Tailor your resume to the company or graduate school you are interviewing with.
- Highlight key words and phrases that are your biggest selling points.

Get References

- Decide who can give you the strongest references.
- Talk to references about possible job leads.
- Inform your references about your strongest selling points.

Research Target Corporations and Graduate Schools

- Investigate typical beginning job activities.
- Look into chance for advancement and career paths
- Assess if company or graduate school meets your needs.
- Develop strategy for expressing match of company's or graduate school's needs to your interests and abilities.
- Apply to graduate or professional schools.

Master the Interviewing Process

- Research typical questions you might be asked.
- Prepare effective questions to ask the interviewer.
- Role play upcoming interviews with friends. Ask for feedback.
- Write down impressions immediately following each interview.
- Send thank-you note to each interviewer.

Take Plant Trips or Visit Grad Schools

- Investigate what happens during the plant trip or in the graduate school selection process.
- Send any requested additional information.

Evaluate Offers

- Determine what your needs are versus what the company or graduate school has to offer.
- Seek guidance, if necessary.
- Choose best offer.

APPENDIX II

TAKE STOCK
IN YOURSELF

Transfer the points you accumulate to the Blue-Chip Portfolio
at the end of this appendix.

O. E.

FRESHMAN YEAR

1. Have you lost an important paper
and then found it later after it is no
longer needed?   YES NO

2. Could you arrange an important
out-of-town trip at a moment's notice
without a scheduling conflict?   YES NO

3. Did you end up pulling a late
nighter at least once this academic
year?   YES NO

4. Did you make below a 60 on at least
one pop test this year?   YES NO

5. Can you name five job opportunities
that are available to someone with
your major?   YES NO

6. Can you list three functional skills
and examples that would convince
an employer that you are a desirable
candidate for summer, co-op, or
part-time employment?   YES NO

7. Can you name five employers who
hire freshmen for summer, co-op or
part-time employment in your
career field?   YES NO

8. Did you do poorly on at least one
test because you were too anxious?   YES NO

1. If you answered YES, your filing system (or lack of one) is inefficient. Read chapter 3, "How to Write a Term Paper, Coordinate Homecoming and Still Have Time to Party." Give yourself 1 point if you answered NO.

2. If you answered NO, you need to brush up on your time management skills. Read chapter 3, "How to Write a Term Paper, Coordinate Homecoming and Still Have Time to Party," for assistance. If you answered YES, give yourself 1 point.

3. Waiting until the last minute to prepare for a test indicates that you could use some study skills advice. See chapter 4, "Making the Grade(s)," for some tried and true methods. Give yourself 1 point if you answered YES.

4. Reviewing after class increases retention and lessens the possibility of doing poorly on a pop test. If you answered YES, you could use some help in this area; refer to chapter 4, "Making the Grade(s)." Give yourself 1 point if you answered NO.

5. If you can't name five job opportunities for your major, how do you know if your major is the right one for you? Reread chapter 5, "Doctor, Lawyer, Chief Executive Officer," to shed some light on majors. If you answered YES, give yourself 1 point.

6. Assessing what you have to offer and making a case for it is the first step in getting a job. If you are having trouble doing this, read chapter 6, "Practice Makes Perfect—The Importance of Work." If you answered YES, give yourself 1 point.

7. If you answered NO, how will you find career-related work while in school? See chapter 6, "Practice Makes Perfect—the Importance of Work," for tips on how to find employers who hire college students. Give yourself 1 point if you anwered YES.

8. Help is available if you are having trouble managing stress. See chapter 9, "Keeping Calm Under Pressure & Making Sense of it All," and chapter 10, "Your Secret Goldmine — Resources on Campus," for tension-reducing techniques and for info on the counseling center. Give yourself 1 point if you answered NO.

TOTAL POINTS

Transfer your total score to the BLUE-CHIP PORTFOLIO

SOPHOMORE YEAR

1. Did you officially declare a major?   YES NO

2. Can you name at least six courses
   that you plan on taking in your
   junior year?   YES NO

3. Can you name one contact you have
   developed through membership in a
   professional association?   YES NO

4. Did you work for at least three
   months in a career-related job?   YES NO

5. Can you name three skills that your
   employer most values in an entry-
   level graduate?   YES NO

6. Have you made a speech or given an
   oral presentation to a group?   YES NO

7. Does your resume include two skills
   examples that you have acquired
   since your freshman year?   YES NO

8. Can you make an effective Five-
   Minute Presentation?   YES NO

1. If you haven't declared a major, it would be worthwhile to seek some career counseling and reread chapter 5, "Doctor, Lawyer, Chief Executive Officer." Give yourself 2 points if you answered YES.

2. If you can't, chances are you haven't clearly thought out which courses you need to take for your major and minor. Talk to your advisor and read chapter 5, "Doctor, Lawyer, Chief Executive Officer," for help. If you answered YES, give yourself 2 points.

3. Contacts are just one of the many benefits a professional association can offer. See chapter 8, "It's Who You Know — Building Contacts." Give yourself 2 points if you answered YES.

4. Employers respond very favorably to graduates who have worked in career-related areas. If you are having trouble finding a job that is career related, read chapter 6, "Practice Makes Perfect — The Importance of Work." Give yourself a pat on the back and 2 points if you answered YES.

5. Selling a product without doing proper market research is difficult. If you know what employers want, then you will know which areas to enhance or develop to make yourself a more attractive job candidate. Read chapter 13, "It's A Jungle Out There." Answering YES has earned you 2 points.

6. Professionals who rise the fastest usually have excellent communications skills. College is a good time to hone your public-speaking and group-management abilities. If you have stage fright or lack of opportunities, read chapter 7, "BPOC (Big People on Campus)," for some helpful advice. Give yourself 2 points if you answered YES.

7. If your resume has not been undated to include acquired skills, you may be cheating yourself out of some job opportunities. For resume help read chapter 14, "Writing a Winning Resume." If your resume is current, you deserve 2 points.

8. Interviewing for information is a great way to clear up any confusion you may have about your chosen field and develop contacts for future job leads. Read chapter 13, "It's a Jungle Out There," for help. If you answered YES, give yourself 2 points.

———————————

TOTAL POINTS

Transfer your total score to the BLUE-CHIP PORTFOLIO

JUNIOR YEAR

1. Can you name one example where you have used your leadership skills this year?　　　　　　YES NO

2. Do you know the entry-level salary range for specialization in your chosen field?　　　　　YES NO

3. Do you know the academic requirements for specialization in your chosen field?　　　　　YES NO

4. Can you name five companies who hire graduates in your field?　　　YES NO

6. Based on your skills and interests, do you know what functional employment areas you are best suited for?　　　　　　　　YES NO

7. Have you interviewed for information with at least three people concerning career or graduate school?　　　　　YES NO

8. Have you listed the pros and cons of a graduate degree in your chosen field?　　　　　　　　YES NO

1. Continued development of your communication and managerial skills will build confidence during the interview and on the job. Read chapter 7, "BPOC (Big Person on Campus)," for some helpful ideas. If you answered YES, give yourself 3 points.

2. Thorough research into the job market for your specialization can help you decide whether it is worth your time and effort. Read chapter 5, "Doctor, Lawyer, Chief Executive Officer," for some clues. If you answered YES, give yourself 3 points.

3. Understanding the required coursework will help you to better understand the nature of the specialization. If you know the academic requirements, give yourself 3 points. If not, read chapter 5, "Doctor, Lawyer, Chief Executive Officer."

4. Is your field as marketable as it was when you first chose it as your major? If you need to make career decisions, now is the time to do so. Read chapter 5, "Doctor, Lawyer, Chief Executive Officer," chapter 10, "Your Secret Goldmine — Resources on Campus," and the section on researching a company in chapter 15, "How to Be a Silver-Tongued Devil." If you answered YES, give yourself 3 points.

5. You still have time to develop skills you are weak in. Unless you know a graduate's typical job activities, how will you know where to start? Read chapter 5, "Doctor, Lawyer, Chief Executive Officer," and the section on researching a company in chapter 15, "How to Be a Silvered-Tongued Devil," for help. Give yourself 3 points if you answered YES.

6. Do you envision yourself working in an isolated laboratory or a hustling-bustling office? If you still have unanswered questions, read chapter 13, "It's a Jungle Out There." If you answered YES, give yourself 3 points.

7. Line up job contacts and increase your understanding of the work environment by interviewing for information. Chapter 8, "It's Who You Know — Building Contacts," is helpful. If you answered YES, you deserve 3 points.

8. A graduate degree doesn't necessarily make you more marketable in all fields. A decision like this deserves a lot of consideration. Chapter 16, "The Blue-Chip Payoff — Choosing the Best Offer" has some good advice. If you answered YES, give yourself 3 points.

_____

TOTAL POINTS

Transfer your total score to the BLUE-CHIP PORTFOLIO

SENIOR YEAR

1. Did you register with the campus placement office? or Did you use any preparatory guides before taking your graduate school entrance exams? (ANSWER ONLY ONE)   YES NO

2. Does your resume include at least three career-related skills using the STAR Technique?   YES NO

3. Did you provide your references with copies of your resume?   YES NO

4. Did you thoroughly research the companies and graduate schools where you applied?   YES NO

5. Did you have answers prepared for at least four to six questions typically asked in an interview?   YES NO

6. Did you send thank-you notes to the appropriate people following your interviews?   YES NO

7. Do you know what to expect during the plant trip? or Do you know what the next steps are after you have submitted your graduate school application? (ANSWER ONLY ONE)   YES NO

8. Did you write down the pros and cons of each offer?   YES NO

1. If you didn't register with the placement office, you have not made full use of a valuable opportunity. Chapter 10, "Your Secret Goldmine — Campus Resources," is helpful. Give yourself 4 points if you answered YES.

2. If your resume is "STARless" by now, you really need to read chapter 14, "The Resume — Packaging the Blue-Chip Graduate" If it sparkles with STAR examples, give yourself 4 points.

3. Shame on you if you didn't provide your references with copies of your resume. Read chapter 8, "It's Who You Know — Building Contacts," for obvious reasons. Give yourself 4 points and move one step closer to the job or school of your choice if you answered YES.

4. How can you convince the right people (including yourself) that where you applied is where you want to be, unless you have thoroughly researched the schools or companies you are interested in. Give yourself 4 points if you answered YES. Chapter 15, "How to Be a Silver-Tongued Devil," can give you some pointers.

5. Being prepared can take some of the anxiety out of a stressful situation. For clues on what to expect in an interview, read chapter 15, "How to Be a Silver-Tongued Devil." Give yourself a big pat on the back and 4 points if you answered YES.

6. Aside from showing courtesy, thank-you notes can reinforce qualifications already mentioned or bring out new ones. Chapter 15, "How to Be a Silver-Tongued Devil" gives examples of thank-you notes that work over-time. You deserve 4 points if you answered YES.

7. Understanding the process is half the battle. If you are confused read chapter 15, "How to Be a Silver-Tongued Devil." If you answered YES, give yourself 4 points.

8. If you answered YES, it shows you put some serious thought into the decision. Give yourself 4 point if you did. If you are having trouble making a decision, read chapter 16, "The Blue-Chip Payoff — Choosing the Best Offer."

TOTAL POINTS

Transfer your total score to the BLUE-CHIP PORTFOLIO

BLUE-CHIP

SHADE THE NUMBER OF BLUE CHIPS
YOU EARN EACH YEAR.

SOPHOMORE

SCORE: _____

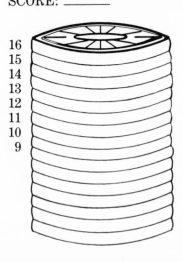

16
15
14
13
12
11
10
9

FRESHMAN

SCORE: _____

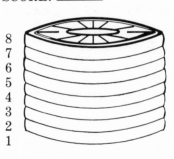

8
7
6
5
4
3
2
1

PORTFOLIO

SUCCESS

SENIOR

SCORE: _____

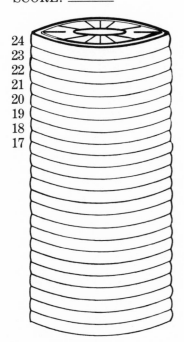

SENIOR	SUCCESS
32	32
31	31
30	30
29	29
28	28
27	27
26	26
25	25
24	24
	23
	22
	21
	20
	19
	18
	17
	16
	15
	14
	13
	12
	11
	10
	9
	8
	7
	6
	5
	4
	3
	2
	1

JUNIOR

SCORE: _____

24
23
22
21
20
19
18
17

APPENDIX III

WHEN TO TRANSFER TO ANOTHER SCHOOL

Back in the late sixties and early seventies some students changed schools almost as often as they changed their underwear. A bit of an exaggeration, but the rate of transfers has gone down as college tuition and living expenses have skyrocketed. Parents are less willing to foot the bill for cross-country coeds. Employers suspect academic nomads of being unfocused and undependable.

Still, there are times when changing schools is in your best interest. You obviously have to transfer if you've finished a junior college program. Sometimes you or your family have to move, and it's impractical to maintain enrollment in your current school. It gets a little trickier when your college experience is somehow not meeting your needs.

What if your university has a great program in your field of interest, but all the social life of a monastary? Or what if you love the school, but they just don't offer the major you want? These are tough decisions, but life is full of them, and blue-chippers don't avoid making decisions.

While there are no perfect colleges, we think most of you can find a school that will meet many of your needs. Don't stay in a school that's wrong for you out of inertia. It may be that your career plans change markedly after your freshman year. Don't stick around for your boyfriend or your fraternity brothers if it means following the wrong career path.

If you're really unhappy where you are, try to pinpoint why. Get some help. Talk with a counselor or advisor.

Consider the following factors during your deliberations:

1. Not enough courses in your area of interest
2. Faculty is weak in your area
3. Graduates have difficulty finding good jobs, or getting into good graduate programs
4. Tuition and fees cost too much
5. Classes too large
6. Want to graduate from a more prestigious school
7. No cooperative plan available
8. Coursework either too difficult or not challenging enough
9. Urban versus small town or rural setting
10. Traditional versus experimental approach to education
11. Religious versus secular atmosphere
12. Small versus large school
13. Institute offering few programs versus university offering many
14. Poor social life
15. Too few fellow blacks, Hispanics, women, etc.
16. Anti-intellectual or unprofessional attitude is prevalent
17. Faculty and staff inaccessible or unresponsive.

No matter why you transfer, you will probably face a period of adjustment. Other students have already formed relationships and study groups. They are already familiar with the campus, what the resources are, who the good profs are. Get involved in an extracurricular activity as soon as possible. It will help you meet people and get your mind off of your insecurities. Many colleges have set up programs dealing specifically with the needs of transfer students. You'll be doing yourself a favor if you take advantage of them.

APPENDIX IV

SHOULD I GET AN ADVANCED DEGREE?

LAW SCHOOL

Admissions:

The most important factors are:

    1. Grades   2. LSAT Scores

Other factors that influence admission:

    3. Personal qualifications and accomplishments

    4. Ethnic group, gender, and geographic diversity

    5. Graduate or professional school record

    6. Letters of recommendation

    7. Relationship with law school (Your chances are better if the library is named after one of your parents.)

LSAT Facts:

Since 1982 a writing sample has been a part of the LSAT. Reading comprehension, analytical reasoning, evaluation of facts, and logical ability are also tested. In 1983-84, 89 percent of students took the test once, 11 percent took it twice, and .4 percent took it three or more times. You can cancel scores before they are reported, but the law schools are notified that you have been exposed to the LSAT. Law schools tend to average scores of repeat test-takers. (Information taken from the 1985-1986 PRELAW HANDBOOK: The Official Guide to U.S. Law Schools.)

How To Get In:

If you decide to go prelaw in college, contact your school's prelaw advisor early on. Join the prelaw club if there is one. Get hold of guides to the LSAT and to Law School. They're full of good information and sound advice. Remember, entrance into a better law school depends on grades and LSAT scores. GPA and LSAT depend on your verbal skills and reasoning ability. Can you read well? Rapidly and with comprehension? Can you write well? With clarity and ease? Are you an analytical thinker? If not, we suggest you think twice about a legal career.

The Job Market For Lawyers

The 1984-1985 OCCUPATIONAL OUTLOOK HANDBOOK projects a moderate demand for lawyers through the nineties. The number graduating from law school has doubled in the last ten years. Naturally, then, competition is keen. Graduates of less prominent law schools will have to struggle. So will those with undistinguished academic records.

Books To Read:

    BARRON'S GUIDE TO LAW SCHOOLS

    BARRON'S GUIDE TO THE NEW LAW SCHOOL

      ADMISSION TEST

    GETTING INTO LAW SCHOOL

      By Amy Shapiro & Sandra W. Weckesser

      Philadelphia: W. B. Saunders Co., 1979

    PRELAW HANDBOOK

      The Official Guide to U.S. Law Schools

      Law School Admission Council

MEDICAL SCHOOL

Admissions:

The most important factors are:
1. Grades   2. MCAT Scores

Other factors influencing admissions are:
3. Personality and character
4. Place of residence
5. Career plans
6. Recommendations
7. Interviews
8. Being a member of a disadvantaged minority group.

Fewer than 10% of those applicants who were admitted had GPAs below a 3.0.

MCAT Facts:

There are six subtests:
1. Reading
2. Quantitative
3. Biology
4. Chemistry
5. Physics
6. Scientific Problem Solving

From: MEDICAL SCHOOL ADMISSION
      REQUIREMENTS, 1983-84
      Association of American Medical Colleges

How To Get In:

The big problem is getting through the door. Good grades from a good school is obviously the key. Master the skills presented in chapters 3 and 4 of this book as soon as possible, preferably by yesterday. Latch onto your pre-med advisor early on. Organic Chemistry and Human Anatomy will probably be your biggest academic hurdles. Unless you're an unusually strong student, we recommend auditing these two courses before you take them for credit. If you're weak in math, get tutorial assistance. A few low grades can torpedo your plans. And don't forget, you'll be tested on Physics and Math on the MCAT.

Finally, we advise having an alternative career plan in the event you don't make it into medical school.

Books To Read:

GETTING INTO MEDICAL SCHOOL
   Donald J. Solomon
   Philadelphia: W.B. Saunders Co., 1979

BARRON'S GUIDE TO MEDICAL, DENTAL, AND ALLIED
   HEALTH SCIENCE CAREERS

MEDICAL SCHOOL ADMISSION REQUIREMENTS, 1983-84
   Association of American Medical Colleges

THE MBA

Admissions:

The major selection criteria are:

1. Grades   2. GMAT Scores
3. Your accomplishments or experience at work, in the military, or in campus or community activities
4. The overall quality of your application and recommendations
5. Intangibles such as your motivation, maturity, and leadership abilities, as suggested by a variety of information.

GMAT Facts:

A four-hour test assessing:

Quantitative — Basic mathematics, quantitative reasoning, problem solving, graph interpretation

Verbal — Reading comprehension, writing ability, analysis of situations.

How To Get In:

To get into a top school, you need top grades. But graduate programs in business tend to weigh practical experience more heavily than do most other graduate programs. Therefore, co-ops and those with internships or career-related summer work will be at an advantage compared with those who have had no significant work history at all. Having clear career plans also counts in your favor. Read the basic books on how to get into an MBA program and go to it.

The Job Market for MBAs

It's good. Which is why the number of MBAs is multiplying faster than your kid brother's gerbil collection. There were 5,000 graduates in 1965, 21,000 in 1970, 45,000 in 1977, and 63,000 in 1983.

Books To Read:

BARRON'S GUIDE TO GRADUATE BUSINESS SCHOOLS

THE OFFICIAL GUIDE TO MBA
    Graduate Management Admission Council

THE MBA CAREER: MOVING ON THE FAST TRACK TO SUCCESS
    Eugene Bronstein & Robert Hisrich
    Barron's Educational Series

OTHER GRADUATE PROGRAMS

Admissions:

The most important factors are:

1. Grades   2. Graduate admissions test scores

Also considered are:

3. Letters of recommendation
4. Appropriateness of undergraduate degree
5. Interview
6. Evidence of creative talent.

Admission Tests:

Graduate Record Exam

General test: Seven 30 minute sections designed to measure verbal, quantitative, and analytical abilities. Think of it as the SAT for college students.

Subject tests: There are 17 different areas, ranging from biology to Spanish. Each test lasts 170 minutes.

Miller Analogies Test: Requires the solution of 100 intellectual problems stated in the form of analogies.

The GRE and the MAT are the most widely used, but there are also:

Dental Admission Testing Program
NTE Program Tests (formerly National Teacher Examinations)
Optometry College Admission Test
Pharmacy College Admission Test.

The Job Market

As we suggested in Chapter 13, it all depends on your field. A PhD in electrical engineering will have many more options to choose from than a PhD in Classics. Some fields require a doctorate. In others, the terminal degree is a master's. Some schools are professional — dental, optometry. Some are research — you're trained to conduct scientific or scholarly research. If you want to be a researcher, it may be less important for you to attend a prestigious school than to study under a famous scholar.

Books to Read

GRADUATE & PROFESSIONAL PROGRAMS,
An Overview 1985, Peterson's Guides

(Also look at the Peterson's Guide specific to your field.)

THE GOURMAN REPORT (provides ratings of the top schools)

APPENDIX V

MORE TO READ

1. WHAT COLLEGE STUDENTS WANT — JOB$

IACOCCA, Lee Iacocca. Bantam, 1984.

IN SEARCH OF EXCELLENCE: Lessons from America's Best-run Companies, Thomas J. Peters and Robert H. Waterman, Jr. Warner, 1982.

*REAL WORLD 101: What College Never Taught You About Success, James Calano and Jeff Salzman. Warner, 1984.

2. WHAT EMPLOYERS WANT — BLUE-CHIP GRADUATES

*JOBS FOR ENGLISH MAJORS AND OTHER SMART PEOPLE, John L. Munschauer. Peterson's Guides, 1982.

MEGATRENDS: Ten New Directions Transforming Our Lives, John Naisbitt. Warner, 1982.

3. HOW TO WRITE A TERM PAPER, COORDINATE HOMECOMING AND STILL HAVE TIME TO PARTY

*GETTING ORGANIZED, The Easy Way to Put Your Life in Order, Stephanie Winston. Norton, 1978.

GETTING THINGS DONE: The ABCs of Time Management, Edwin C. Bliss. Bantam, 1980.

HOW TO GET CONTROL OF YOUR TIME AND YOUR LIFE, Alan Lakein. New American Library, 1974.

WORKING SMART: How to Accomplish More in Half the Time, Michael LeBoeuf. Warner, 1980.

4. MAKING THE GRADE(S)

*BECOMING A MASTER STUDENT (5th Ed.), David B. Ellis. College Survival Press, 1986.

*HOW TO STUDY IN COLLEGE (3rd Ed.), Walter Pauk. Houghton Mifflin, 1984.

HOW TO SUCCEED IN COLLEGE, Marcia K. Johnson, Sally P. Springer, and Sarah Hall Sternglanz. William Kaufmann, Inc., 1982.

STUDYING SMART, Diana Scharf, Ph.D. Harper & Row, 1985.

STUDY SKILLS FOR SUCCESS: How to Learn Effectively, William M. Saleebey. National Publishers, 1984.

USE BOTH SIDES OF YOUR BRAIN, Tony Buzan. Dutton, 1983.

YOUR NUMBER'S UP: A Calculated Approach to Successful Math Study, C. Ann Oxrieder and Janet P. Ray. Addison-Wesley, 1982.

5. DOCTOR, LAWYER, CHIEF EXECUTIVE OFFICER

CHOOSING A CAREER IN BUSINESS, Stephen A. Stumpf, Ph.D. Simon & Schuster, 1984.

DREAM JOBS: A Guide to Tomorrow's Top Careers, Robert W. Bly and Gary Blake. John Wiley & Sons, 1983.

ENGINEERING/HIGH-TECH STUDENT'S HANDBOOK: Preparing for Careers of the Future, David R. Reyes-Guerra and Alan M. Fischer. Peterson's Guides, 1985.

WORKING, Studs Terkel. Ballantine, 1985.

6. PRACTICE MAKES PERFECT — THE IMPORTANCE OF WORK

GETTING WORK EXPERIENCE: The College Students' Directory of Summer Internship Programs That Lead to Careers, Betsy Bauer. Dell, 1985.

FOREIGN JOBS: The Most Popular Countries, Curtis W. Casewit. Monarch Press, 1984.

*MAKING COLLEGE PAY: How to Earn Money While You're Still in School, Jon E. Carson. Addison-Wesley, 1983.

1987 INTERNSHIPS: 35,000 On-the-Job Training Opportunities For All Types of Careers, Katherine Jobst, ed. Writer's Digest Books, updated annually.

1987 SUMMER EMPLOYMENT DIRECTORY OF THE UNITED STATES, Pat Beusterian, ed. Writer's Digest Books, updated annually.

*THE STUDENT ENTREPRENEUR'S GUIDE, Brett Kingstone. Ten Speed Press, 1981.

7. BPOC (BIG PERSON ON CAMPUS)

CONQUERING COLLEGE LIFE: How to be a Winner at College, Lawrence Graham. Washington Square Press, 1983.

8. IT'S WHO YOU KNOW — BUILDING CONTACTS

THE HIDDEN JOB MARKET FOR THE 80s, Tom Jackson and Davidyne Mayleas. Times Books, 1981.

SHYNESS: What It Is. What to Do About It. Philip G. Zimbardo. Berkley Publishing Group, 1985.

WHAT COLOR IS YOUR PARACHUTE? Richard Nelson Bolles. Ten Speed Press, 1986 (revised annually).

236

9. KEEPING CALM UNDER PRESSURE & MAKING SENSE OF IT ALL

COPING WITH DIFFICULT PEOPLE . . . in Business and in Life, Robert M. Bramson, Ph.D. Ballantine, 1983.

DEALING WITH CRISIS: A Guide to Critical Life Problems, Lawrence G. Calhoun, James W. Selby, and H. Elizabeth King. Prentice-Hall, 1976.

HOW TO SURVIVE A ROOMMATE: Two Can Live Better Than One (If They Don't Kill Each Other First!), James Comer. Franklin Watts, 1980.

*A NEW GUIDE TO RATIONAL LIVING, Albert Ellis and Robert A. Harper. Wilshire, 1975.

STRESS WITHOUT DISTRESS, Hans Selye, M.D. New American Library, 1974.

10. YOUR SECRET GOLDMINE — RESOURCES ON CAMPUS

COLLEGE 101, Ronald T. Farrar. Peterson's Guides, 1984.

HOW THE MILITARY WILL HELP YOU PAY FOR COLLEGE, Don M. Betterton. Peterson's Guides, 1985.

HOW TO SUCCEED IN COLLEGE, Marcia K. Johnson, Sally P. Springer, and Sarah Hall Sternglanz. William Kaufmann, Inc., 1982.

THE 1987 COLLEGE MONEY HANDBOOK, Karen C. Hegener, ed. Peterson's Guides, 1986 (updated annually).

11. WHAT MAKES ACHIEVERS TICK?

THE ACHIEVEMENT MOTIVE, David C. McClelland. Irvington, 1976.

THE ACHIEVING SOCIETY, David C. McClelland. Van Nostrand, 1961.

DOING IT NOW, Edwin C. Bliss. Bantam, 1983.

12. DOCTOR, LAWYER, CHIEF EXECUTIVE OFFICER: THE SEQUEL

THE DAMN GOOD RESUME GUIDE, Yana Parker. Ten Speed Press, 1983.

THE NEW QUICK JOB-HUNTING MAP, Richard Nelson Bolles. Ten Speed Press, 1986.

13. IT'S A JUNGLE OUT THERE

THE ALMANAC OF AMERICAN EMPLOYERS: A Guide to America's 500 Most Successful Large Corporations, Jack W. Plunkett. Contemporary Books, 1985.

BUSINESS & MANAGEMENT JOBS. Peterson's Guides, updated annually.

*THE COMPLETE JOB-HUNTING GUIDE FOR COLLEGE STUDENTS, Lawrence J. Danks. Prentice-Hall, 1985.

ENGINEERING, SCIENCE & COMPUTER JOBS. Peterson's Guides, updated annually.

GUERRILLA TACTICS IN THE JOB MARKET, Tom Jackson. Bantam, 1978.

THE HIDDEN JOB MARKET FOR THE 80s, Tom Jackson and Davidyne Mayleas. Times Books, 1981.

JOB HUNTING FOR THE DISABLED, Edith Marks and Adele Lewis. Barron's Educational Series, 1983.

*JOBS FOR ENGLISH MAJORS AND OTHER SMART PEOPLE, John L. Munschauer. Peterson's Guides, 1982.

THE 100 BEST COMPANIES TO WORK FOR IN AMERICA, Robert Levering, Milton Moskowitz and Michael Katz. New American Library, 1985.

WHAT COLOR IS YOUR PARACHUTE? Richard Nelson Bolles. Ten Speed Press, 1986 (revised annually).

14. WRITING A WINNING RESUME

THE COMPLETE JOB-HUNTING GUIDE FOR COLLEGE STUDENTS, Lawrence J. Danks. Prentice-Hall, 1985.

THE DAMN GOOD RESUME GUIDE, Yana Parker. Ten Speed Press, 1983.

LIBERAL ARTS POWER: How to Sell It on Your Resume, Burton Jay Nadler. Peterson's Guides, 1985.

15. HOW TO BE A SILVER-TONGUED DEVIL

*THE COMPLETE JOB-HUNTING GUIDE FOR COLLEGE STUDENTS, Lawrence J. Danks. Prentice-Hall, 1985.

HOW TO SELL YOURSELF ON AN INTERVIEW, Arthur R. Pell, Ph.D. Monarch, 1982.

*SWEATY PALMS: The Neglected Art of Being Interviewed, H. Anthony Medley. Ten Speed Press, 1984.

16. WHICH OFFER TO ACCEPT

*THE COMPLETE JOB-HUNTING GUIDE FOR COLLEGE STUDENTS, Lawrence J. Danks. Prentice-Hall, 1985.

APPENDIX IV. WHEN TO TRANSFER COLLEGES

GUIDE TO FOUR-YEAR COLLEGES, Andrea E. Lehman, ed. Peterson's Guides, revised annually.

APPENDIX V. SHOULD I GET AN ADVANCED DEGREE?

BARRON'S GUIDE TO LAW SCHOOLS, Epstein, Shostak and Troy. Barron's Educational Series, 1984.

THE INSIDER'S GUIDE TO THE TOP TEN BUSINESS SCHOOLS, Tom Fischgrund, ed. Little, Brown, 1985.

LOVEJOY'S SHORTCUTS & STRATEGIES FOR THE LSAT (2ND ED.), David Tajgman, J.D. Monarch, 1985.

MEDICAL SCHOOL ADMISSION REQUIREMENTS — 1987-88. Association of American Medical Colleges.

SHORTCUTS AND STRATEGIES FOR THE GMAT, Gary R. Gruber, Ph.D. Monarch, 1982.

*Highly recommended reading

ACKNOWLEDGMENTS

More thanks than we can adequately express on this page go to our spouses:

Diane Thomas, whose quality of writing is so high I can only dream of approximating it. She supported, edited, advised, and encouraged me throughout this project.

Tom Campbell, a talented and creative writer, whose editorial assistance, hot coffee, and hugs kept me going.

We also thank Dr. Gayle Roberts, a talented psychologist from Georgia Tech, for her expertise and encouragement and for being such a good pal.

Also thanks to family and friends who listened and helped in countless ways: Ida Henley; Walter Henley; Clara Osher; Lucy and Robert Burdine; the members of the Atlanta Midtown Fiction Writers Group (which now meets in Decatur), especially Irene Jurczyk; the staff of the Georgia Tech Counseling & Career Planning Center, especially our director, Dr. Barbara Winship, and our valued secretaries, Barbara Winters and Virginia Cooper; and Vice-President of Student Affairs at Georgia Tech, James Dull.

Appreciation for expert information is extended to: Joan McCarty, Dr. Bill Gamble, Juanita Lloyd, Jo Ivey, Dr. Carole Moore, Bill Hitch and Tom Akins.

Among many librarians who came through for us, these stand out: Stephen Hurd, Gardner Neeley, John Sherman, and Karen Powell.

Thanks for computer assistance to Robert Burdine and Mike Furman, who helped us to teach our computers that we are smarter than they are.

Special gratitude to our students at Georgia Tech who participated in our first Blue-Chip Seminars. You taught us a lot.

ABOUT THE AUTHORS

BILL OSHER was born in Rocky Ford, Colorado. He attended college in Texas, graduating with a B.A. from Southwestern University. He also earned a B.D. from Southern Methodist University. In 1970 he received a Ph.D. in counseling psychology from the University of Texas in Austin. Osher was formerly employed as a counseling psychologist at the Center for Psychological Services at Ohio University. He now serves as Associate Director of Counseling and Career Planning at Georgia Tech. He has written numerous articles on assertiveness and sports psychology.

Osher and his wife now live in Decatur, Georgia. Their son is a "Blue-Chip" journalism student at the University of Arkansas.

SIOUX HENLEY CAMPBELL, born in Tuscaloosa, Alabama, put herself through school while also supporting her young son. She graduated in 1982 with a B.A. in Communications from the University of Alabama. Now a career information specialist at the Georgia Institute of Technology, she also teaches a "Fresh Start Seminar" to faculty spouses who plan to reenter the work force.

Campbell and her husband and two sons reside in Decatur, Georgia.